PIANO **VOCAL** GUITAR

CHART HITS OF '98-'99

TWENTY-SIX
OF TODAY'S
POP FAVORITES IN
ONE COLLECTION!

P9-DDV-759

ISBN 0-634-00516-2

HAL•LEONARD®
CORPORATION

7777 W. BLUEMOUND RD. P.O. BOX 13819 MILWAUKEE, WI 53213

Visit Hal Leonard Online at
www.halleonard.com

CHART HITS OF '98-'99

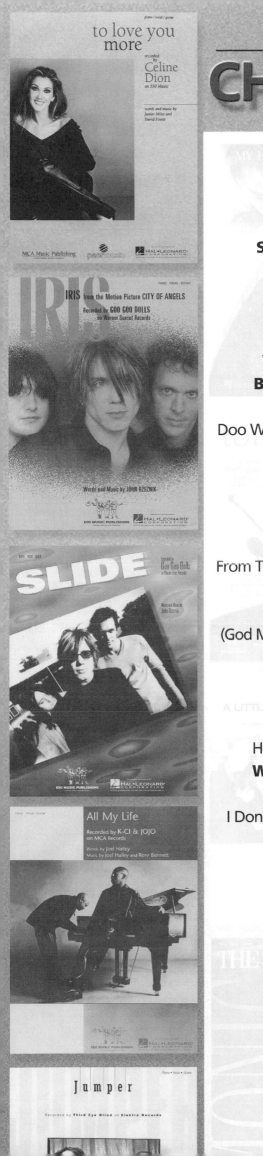

ALL MY LIFE

Words by JOEL HAILEY
Music by JOEL HAILEY and RORY BENNETT

Original key: D♭ major. This edition has been transposed down one half-step to be more playable.

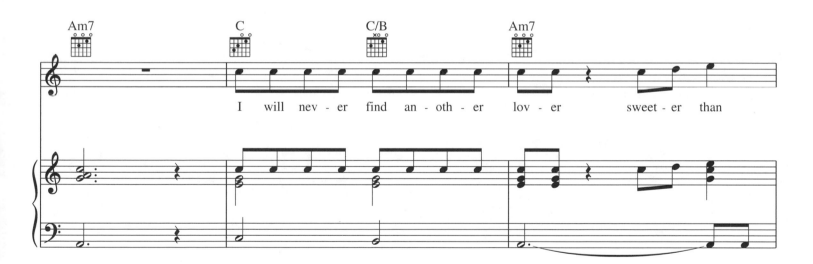

I will nev - er find an - oth - er lov - er sweet - er than

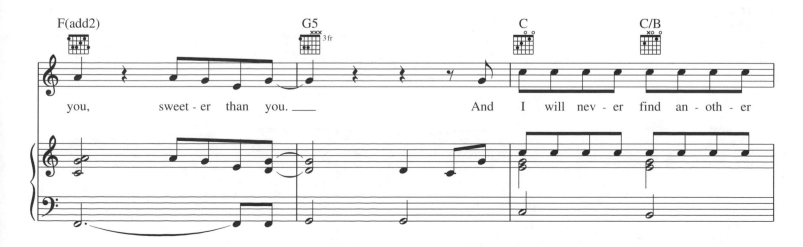

you, sweet - er than you. ____ And I will nev - er find an - oth - er

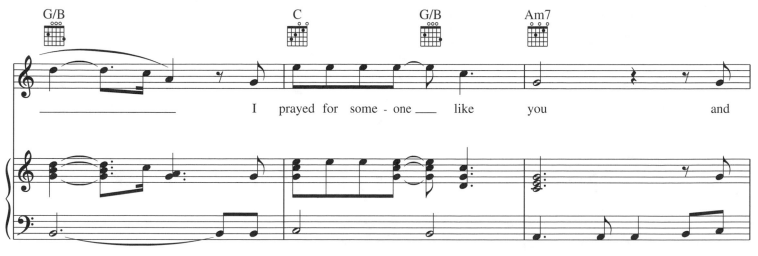

I prayed for some - one ___ like you ___ and

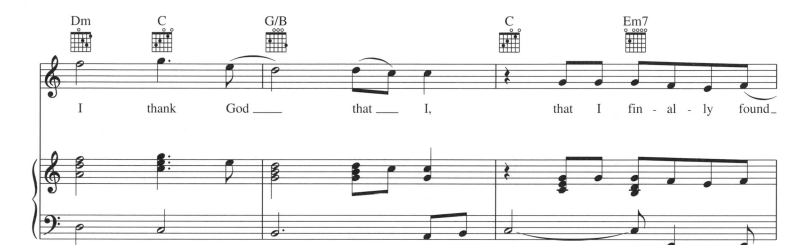

I thank God ___ that ___ I, that I fin - al - ly found ___

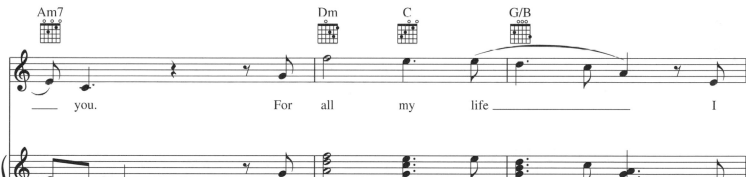

___ you. For all my life ___ I

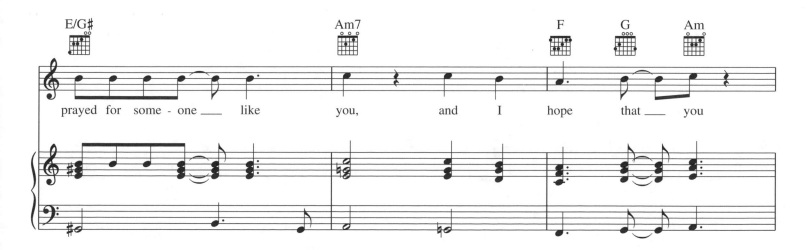

prayed for some - one ___ like you, and I hope that ___ you

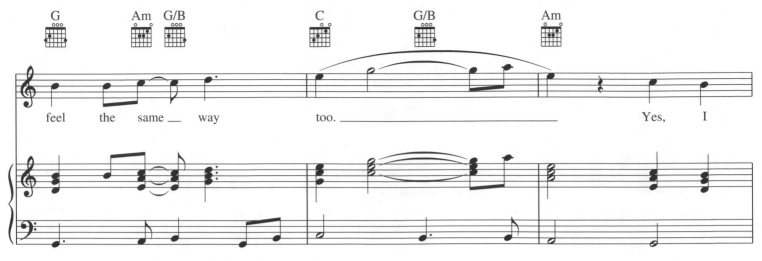

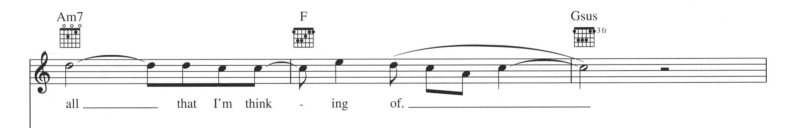

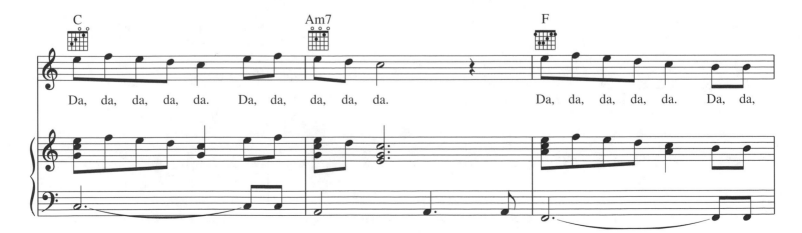

-er know. When you smile ___ on my face, ___ all I see ___ is a glow. You turned ___

___ my life ___ a - round. You picked ___ me up ___ when I ___ was down.

___ You're all that I ev - er know. When you smile life is glow.

You picked me up when I was down. Say'n you're all that I ev - er know.

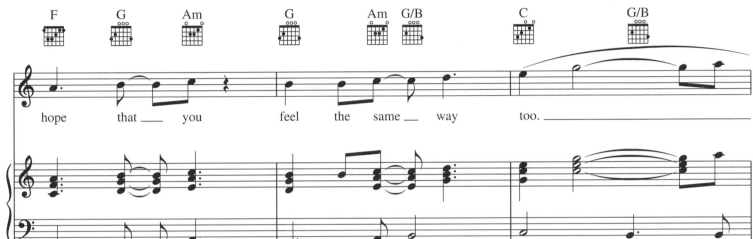

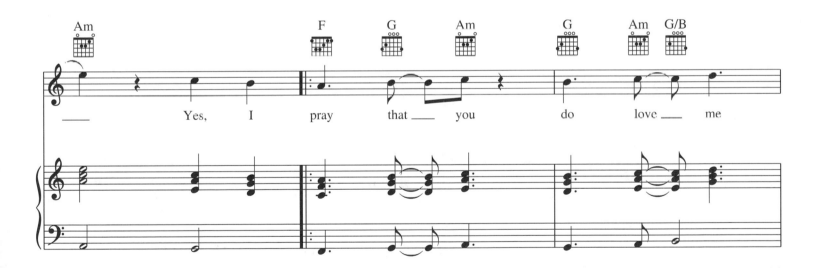

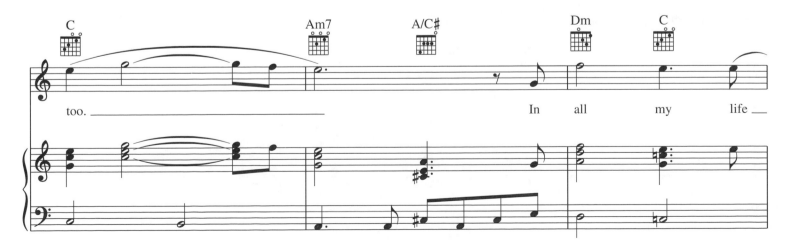

ANGEL OF MINE

Words and Music by TRAVON POTTS
and RHETT LAWRENCE

Easy R & B Ballad

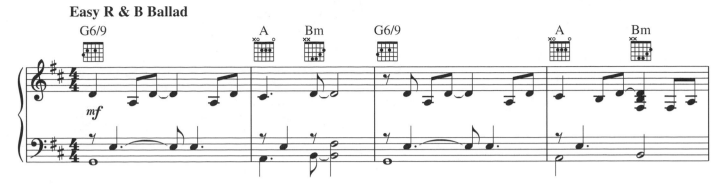

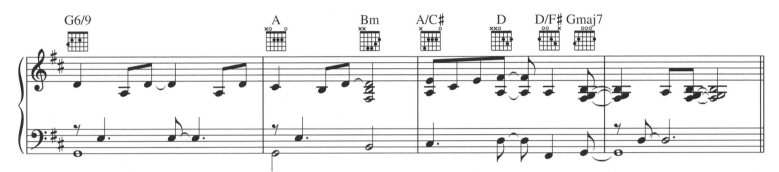

When I first saw you I al-read-y knew _____ there was some-thing

in-side _ of you, some-thing I thought that I would nev-er find, __

Original key: D♭ major. This edition has been transposed up one half-step to be more playable.

%

A/C# · D · D/F# Gmaj7 · G6/9 · A · Bm

an - gel _ of _ mine. _
I look at you _ look-ing at me. ____
Noth-in' means more to me than what _ we share. __
When I first saw you I al-read-y knew ___

G6/9 · A · Bm · G6/9

Now I know why they say the best things _ are _ free. _____
No one in this whole world can ev - er _ com - pare. _____
there was some-thing _ in - side _ of _ you, _____

I'm gon-na love you. Boy, you
Last night the way _ you moved is
some-thing I thought that _ I would

To Coda ⊕

A · Bm · A/C# · D · D/F# Gmaj7 · Em7

are so fine, _____ an - gel of _ mine. ___
still on my mind, _____ an - gel of _ mine. ___
nev - er find, _____ an - gel of _ mine. _.

How you changed my world you'll
What you mean to me you'll

F#7 · F#7#5 · Gmaj7 · C

nev - er know. _____ I'm dif-f'rent now. __ You helped me grow. _____ { You
nev - er know. _____ Deep in - side __ I need to show. _____ } You

that I take, ___ the love ___ that we make, _____ I on-ly share it with you, _

you, you, _ you.

You came in-to my life

sent from a-bove. _ When I lost all hope, you showed me love, _ uh huh. _

___ I'm check-in' for you. Boy, you're right on time, _ an-gel of mine. _

ANGEL

Words and Music by
SARAH McLACHLAN

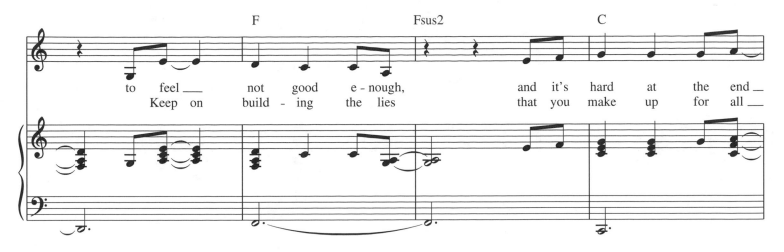

to feel ___ not good e - nough, and it's hard at the end ___
Keep on build - ing the lies that you make up for all ___

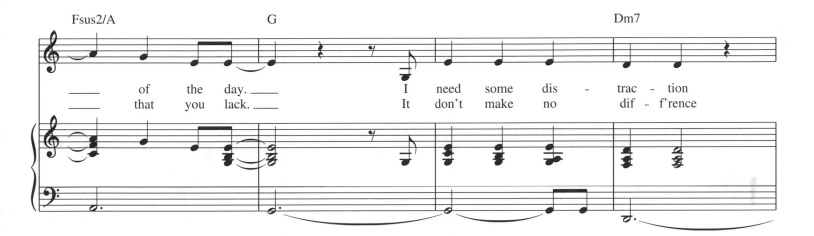

___ of the day. ___ I need some dis - trac - tion
___ that you lack. ___ It don't make no dif - f'rence

oh ___ beau - ti - ful re - lease. ___ Mem - o - ry
es - cap - ing one last time. ___ It's eas - i - er

seep from my ___ veins. Let me be emp - ty
to be - lieve in this sweet mad - ness,

oh and weight - less and may - be I'll find some
oh this glo - ri - ous sad - ness that brings me

peace to - night ___ in the arms of the an -
to my knees ___

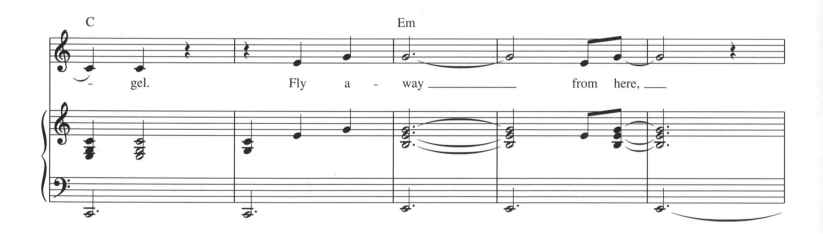

\- gel. Fly a - way _____ from here, ___

from this dark, cold _____ ho - tel room

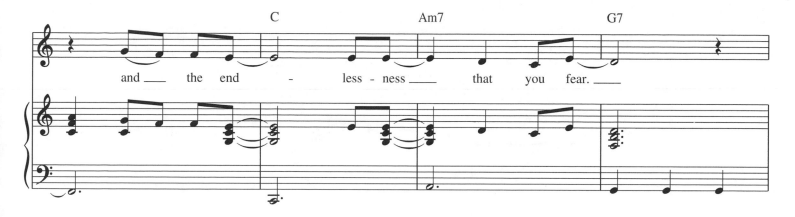

and ___ the end - less - ness ___ that you fear. ___

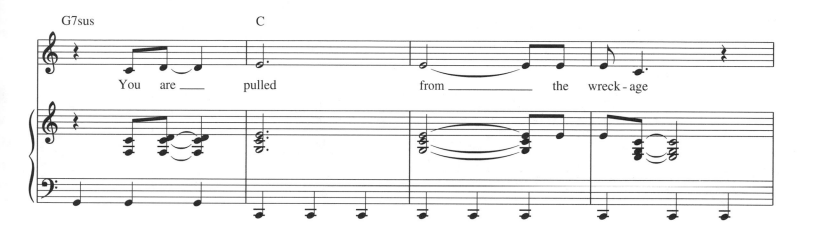

You are ___ pulled from ___ the wreck - age

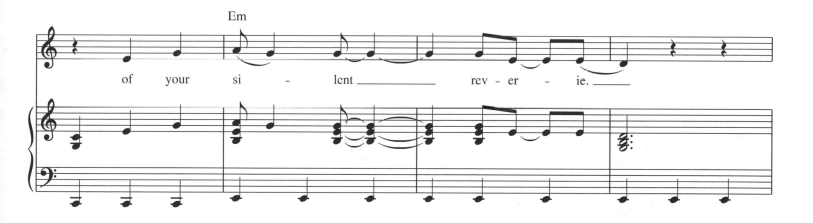

of your si - lent ___ rev - er - ie. ___

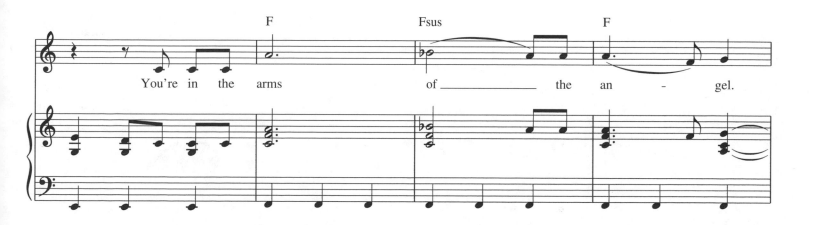

You're in the arms of ___ the an - gel.

22

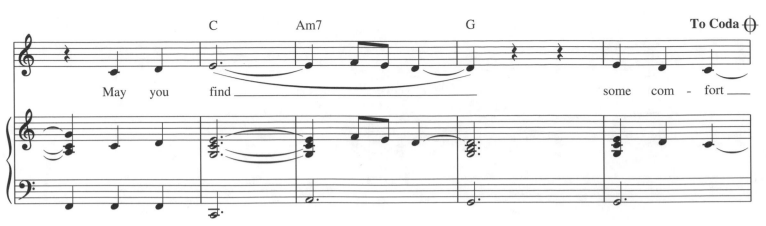

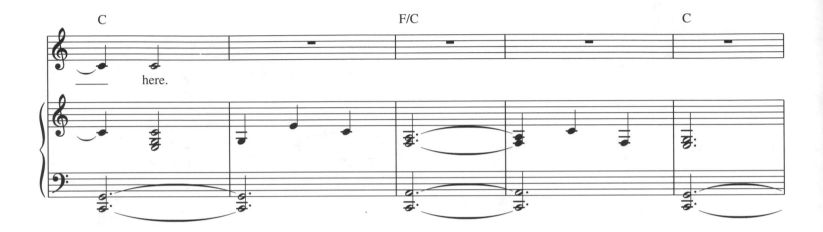

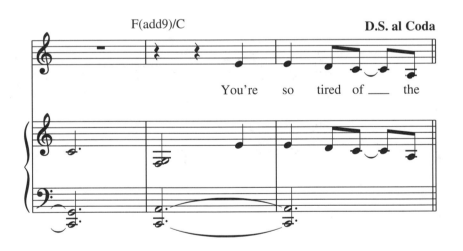

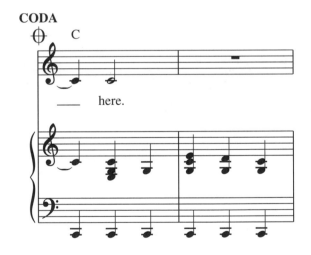

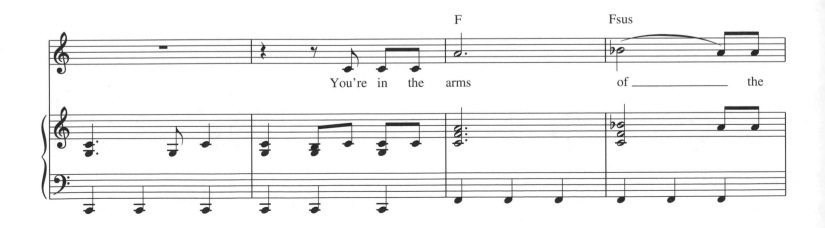

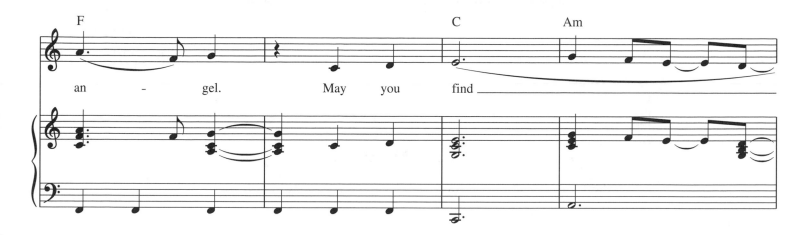

an - gel. May you find _____

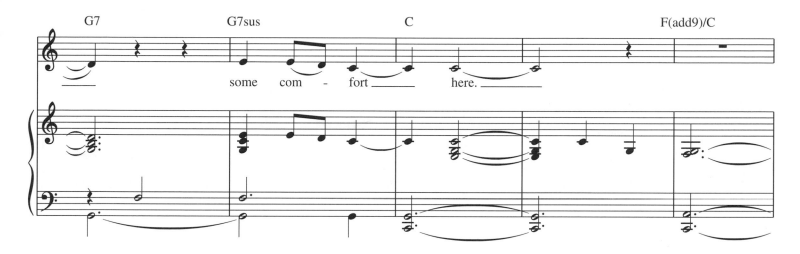

some com - fort _____ here. _____

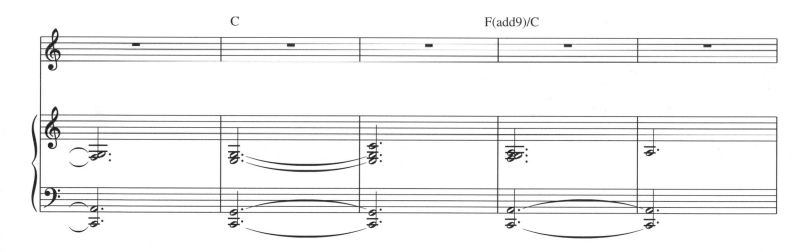

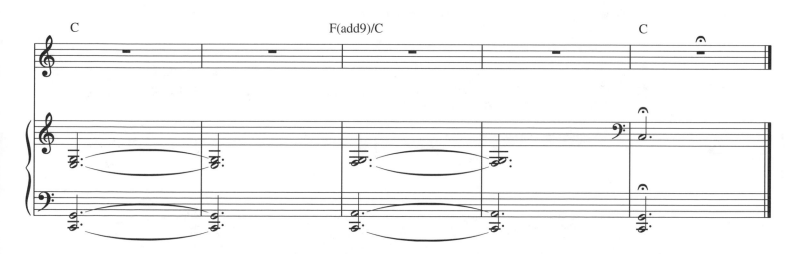

THE BOY IS MINE

Words and Music by LaSHAWN DANIELS,
JAPHE TEJEDA, RODNEY JERKINS,
FRED JERKINS and BRANDY NORWOOD

Moderately fast

Brandy: Excuse me, can I please talk to you for a minute?   *Monica: Uh huh, sure. You know,*

you look kind of familiar. Brandy: Yeah, you do too. But, um, I just wanted to know, do you know

FROM THIS MOMENT ON

Words and Music by SHANIA TWAIN
and R.J. LANGE

*Male vocals sung an octave higher throughout.

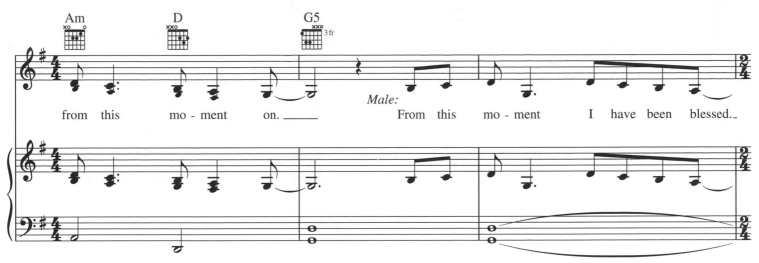

from this mo - ment on. _____ *Male:* From this mo - ment I have been blessed. _

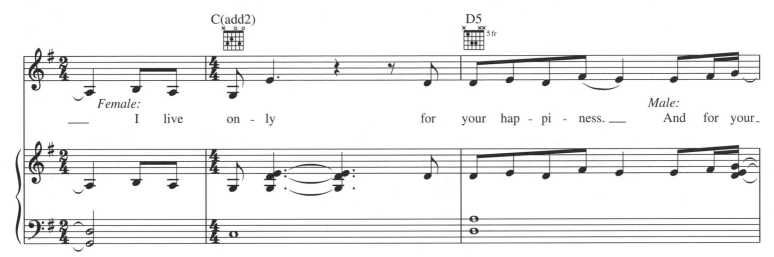

Female: ___ I live on - ly for your hap - pi - ness. _ *Male:* And for your_

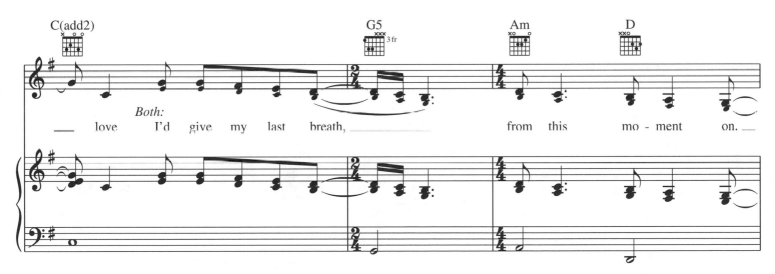

___ love I'd give my last breath, ___ *Both:* from this mo - ment on. _

Female: I give my hand _ to you _ with all _ my heart. _____ *Male:* Can't

prom - ise you this. _____ There is noth - ing I would - n't give, _____

from this mo - ment on. ____

Female: You're the rea - son I ___ be - lieve _ in

love, _____ *Male:* and you're the an - swer to ___ my prayers _ from

up a - bove. _____ *Both:* All we need _____ is just _____ the two _____ of

us. _____ My dreams _____ came true _____ be - cause_

_____ of you. _____ From this

mo - ment, as long as I live, _____ I _____ will

DOO WOP
(That Thing)

Written by
LAURYN HILL

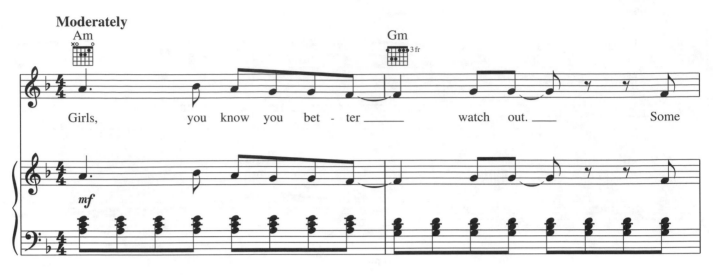

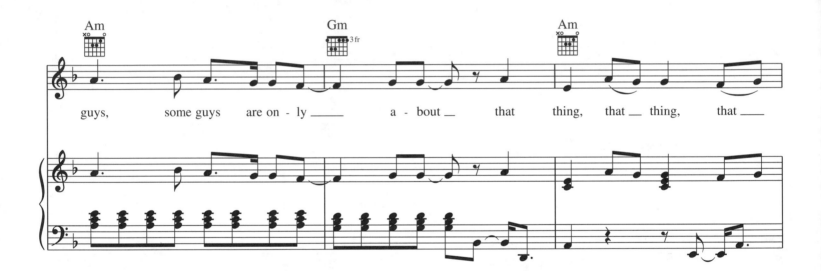

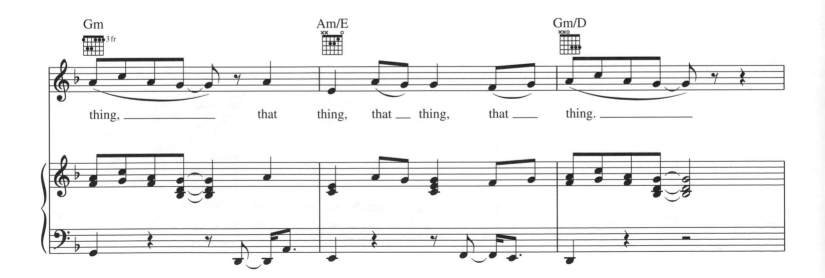

Yeah, yeah. ___   Yeah, yeah. ___   Yeah, yeah. ___

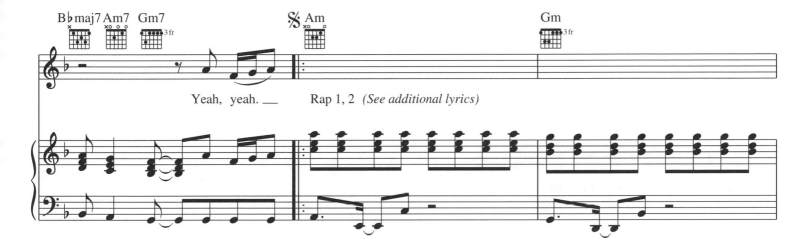

Yeah, yeah. ___   Rap 1, 2 *(See additional lyrics)*

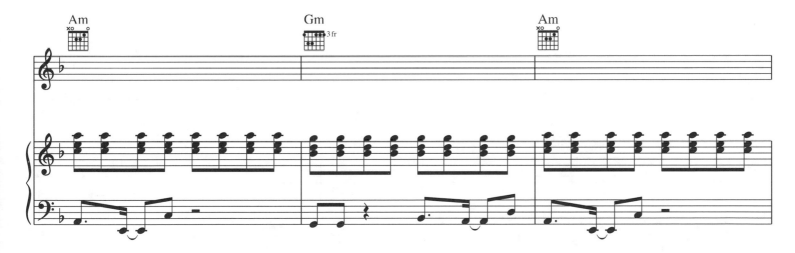

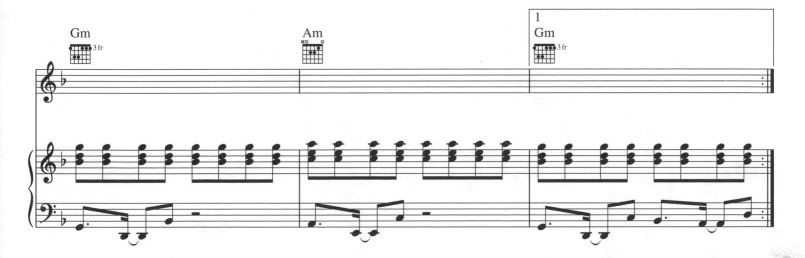

gain. Yeah, yeah. __ Guys, you know you bet - ter __ watch out. __ Some

girls, some girls are on - ly __ a - bout __ that thing, that __ thing, that __

D.S. al Coda

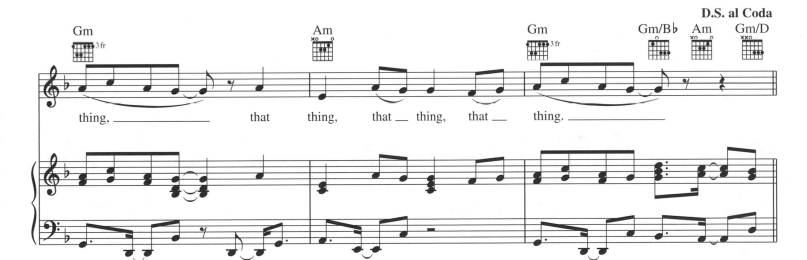

thing, _____ that thing, that __ thing, that __ thing. _____

CODA

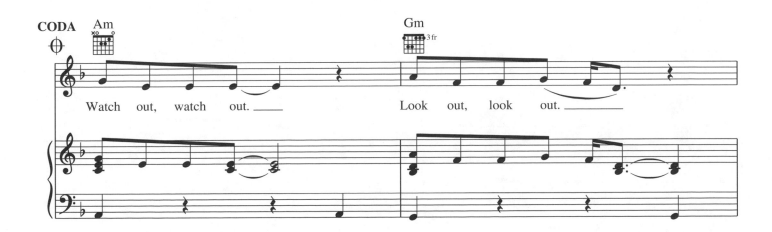

Watch out, watch out. __ Look out, look out. _____

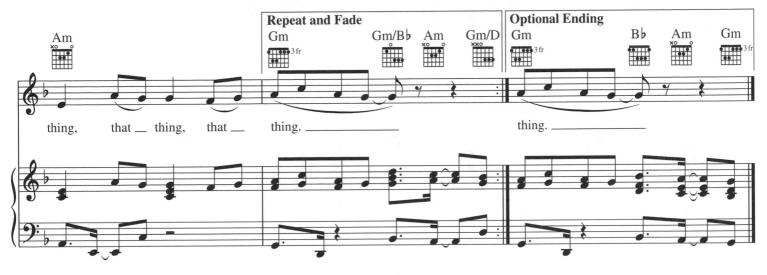

thing,   that __ thing,   that __   thing. _____   thing. _____

Additional Lyrics

Rap 1:   It's been three weeks since you've been lookin' for your friend,
The one you let hit it and never called you again.
'Member when he told you he was 'bout the Benjamins.
You act like you ain't hear him, then give 'em a little trim.
To Begin, how you think you really gon' pretend?
Like you wasn't down, then you called him again.

Plus when, you give it up so easy you ain't even foolin' him.
If you did it then, then you probably fuck again.
Talkin' out your neck sayin' you're a Christian,
A Muslim sleepin' wit' the gin.
Now that was the sin that did Jezabel in.
Who you gon' tell when repercussion spin?

Showin' off your ass 'cause you're thinkin' it's a trend.
Girlfriend, let me break it down for you again.
You know I only say it 'cause I'm truly genuine.
Don't be a hard rock when you really a gem.
Baby girl, respect is just the minimum.
Niggas fucked up and you still defendin' 'em.

Now, Lauryn is only human.
Don't think I haven't been through the same predicament.
Let it sit inside your head like a million in Philly Penn.
It's silly when girls sell their souls because it's in. Look at where you bein.
Hair weaves like Europeans, fake nails done by Koreans.

Rap 2:   The second verse is dedicated to the men
More concerned wit' his rims and his timbs than his women.
Him and his men come in the cub like hooligans.
Don't care who they defend, popping Yang like you got yen.

Let's not pretend,
They wanna pack pistol by they waist men.
Cristal by the case men, still they in they mother's basement.
The pretty face men claimin' that they did a bid men.
Need to take care of their three and four kids, men.

They facin' court case when the child support's late.
Money takin', heart breakin. Now you wonder why women hate men.
And the sneaky, silent men, the punk domestic violence men.
The quick to shoot the semen stop actin' like boys and be men.

How you gon' win when you ain't right within? *(3x's)*
Uh-uh, come again.

THE FIRST NIGHT

Words and Music by TAMARA SAVAGE, JERMAINE DUPRI,
MARILYN McLEOD and PAMELA SAWYER

Original key: E♭ minor. This edition has been transposed down one half-step to be more playable.

*Vocal written one octave higher than sung.

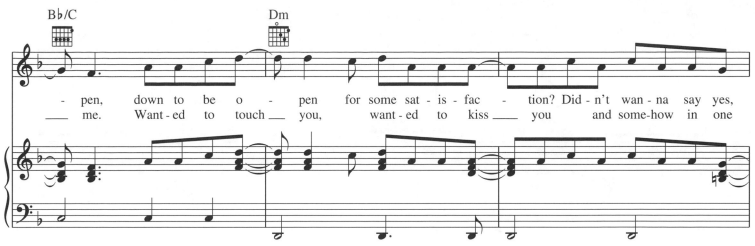

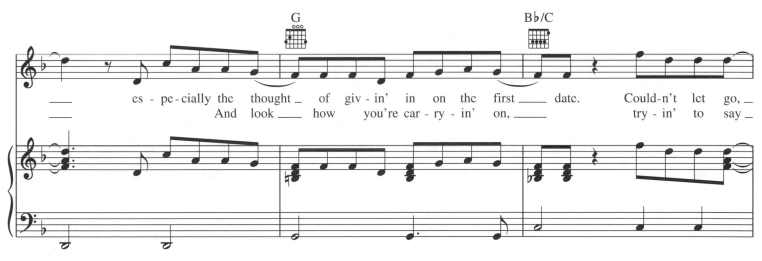

I was / I'm think - in', _____ I should make a move, but I won't. I know you're

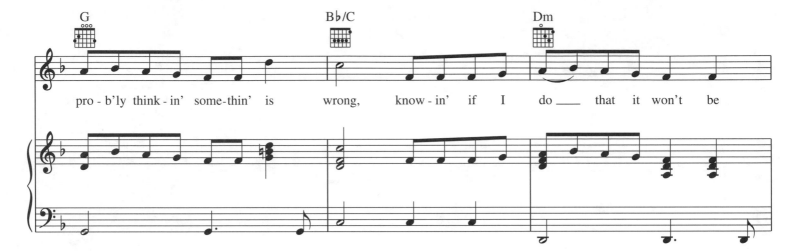

pro - b'ly think - in' some - thin' is wrong, know - in' if I do _____ that it won't be

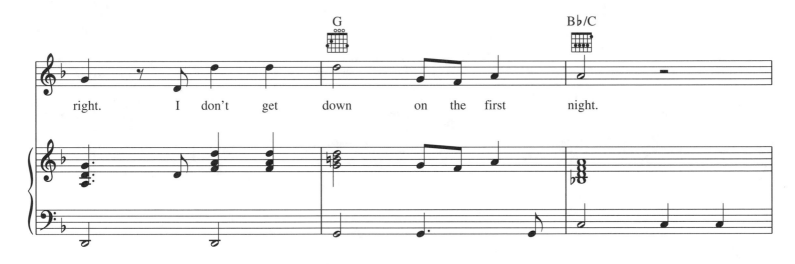

right. I don't get down on the first night.

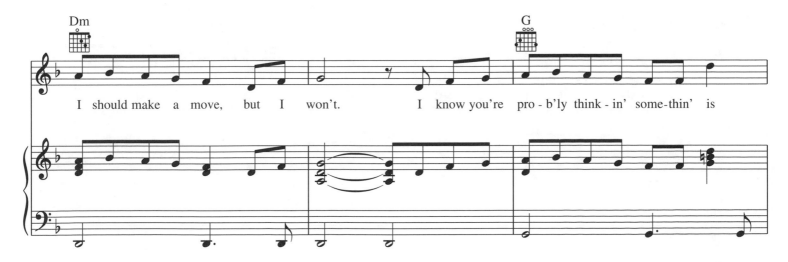

I should make a move, but I won't. I know you're pro - b'ly think - in' some - thin' is

wrong, know-in' if I do ___ that it won't be right. I wan-na get

down, but not the first night. ___
Oh, we're chill - ___ night. ___

If you ___ want ___ me ___ you got ___

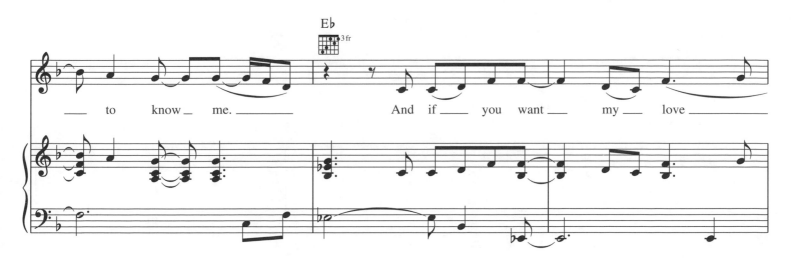

___ to know ___ me. ___ And if ___ you want ___ my ___ love ___

you got - ta wait, __ my __ love. _____ Ba - ba -

- by, _____ that's __ the way __ it's got __ to be. __

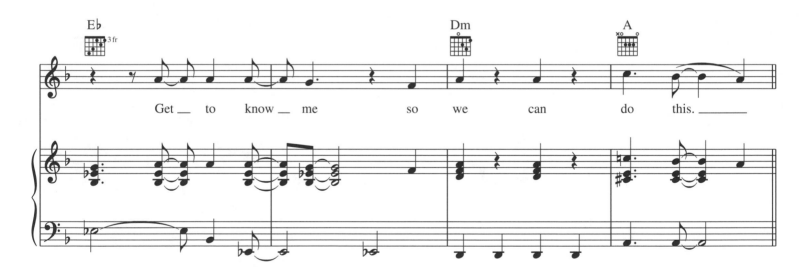

Get __ to know __ me so we can do this. _____

I should make a move, but I won't. I know you're pro - b'ly think - in' some - thin' is
Lead vocal-ad lib.

wrong, know-in' if I do ___ that it won't be right. I don't get

down on the first night. I should make a move, but I won't. I know you're

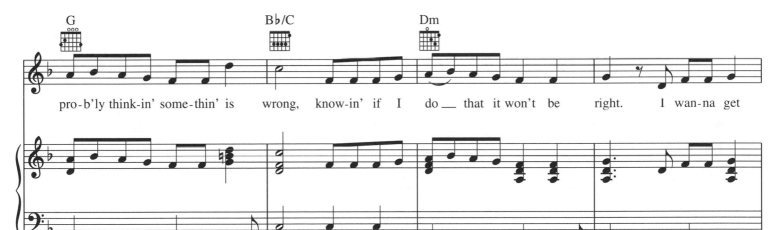

pro-b'ly think-in' some-thin' is wrong, know-in' if I do ___ that it won't be right. I wan-na get

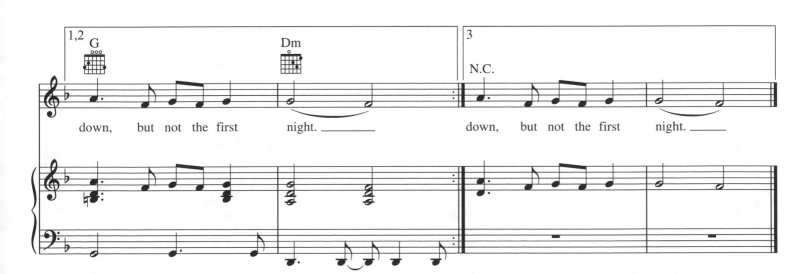

down, but not the first night. ___ down, but not the first night. ___

(God Must Have Spent)
A LITTLE MORE TIME ON YOU

Words and Music by CARL STURKEN
and EVAN ROGERS

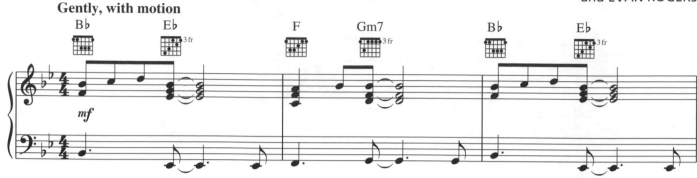

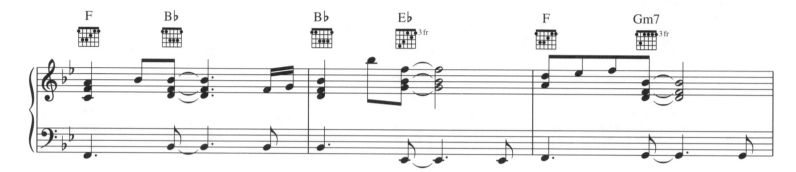

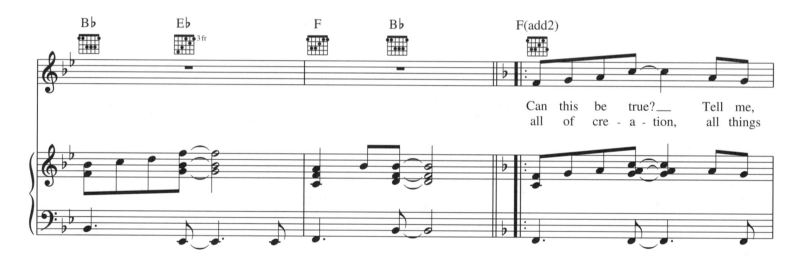

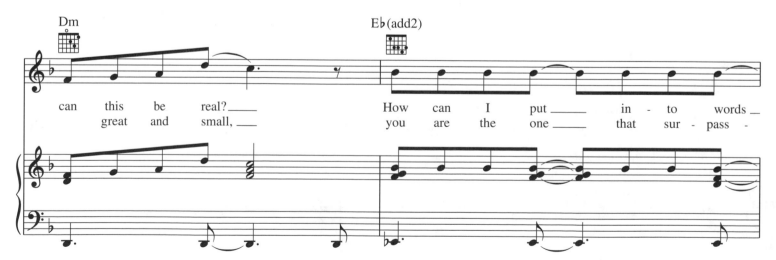

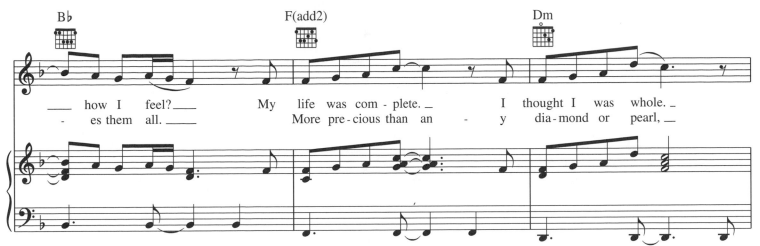

how I feel?___ My life was com-plete.___ I thought I was whole. ___
- es them all. ___ More pre-cious than an - y dia-mond or pearl, ___

Why do I feel ___ like I'm los - ing con-trol?___ I nev - er
they broke the mold ___ when you came ___ in this world. ___ And I'm

1., 3. thought that love could feel ___ like this ___ and you
2. try - in' hard to fig - ure out ___ just

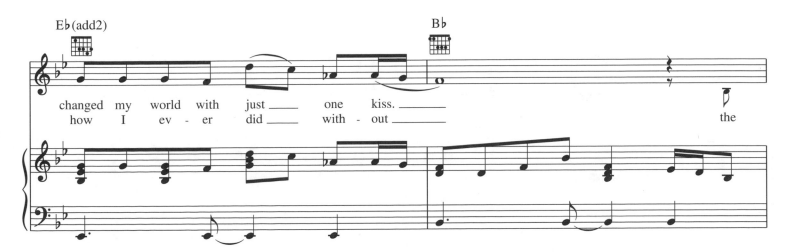

changed my world with just ___ one kiss. ___
how I ev - er did ___ with - out ___ the

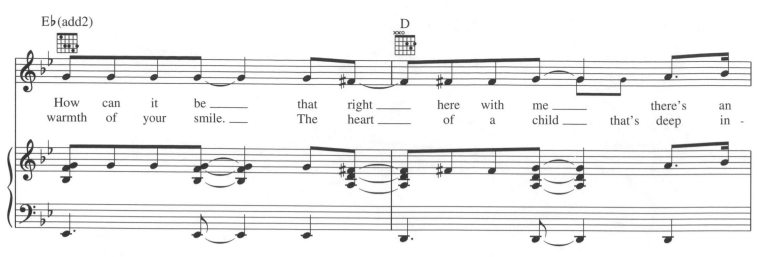

How can it be _____ that right _____ here with me _____ there's an
warmth of your smile. _____ The heart _____ of a child _____ that's deep in -

an - gel? It's a mir - a - cle. _____
side _____ leaves me pur - i - fied. _____

Your love is like a riv - er,

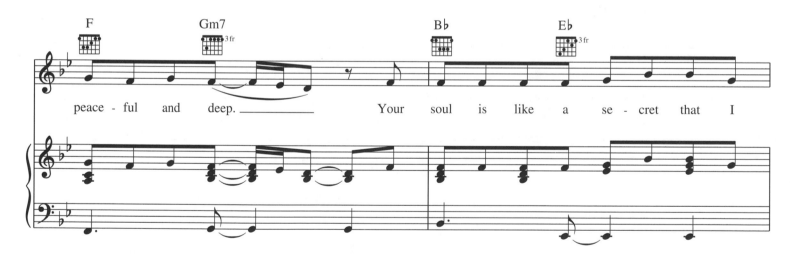

peace - ful and deep. _____ Your soul is like a se - cret that I

nev - er could keep. _____ When I look in - to your eyes I

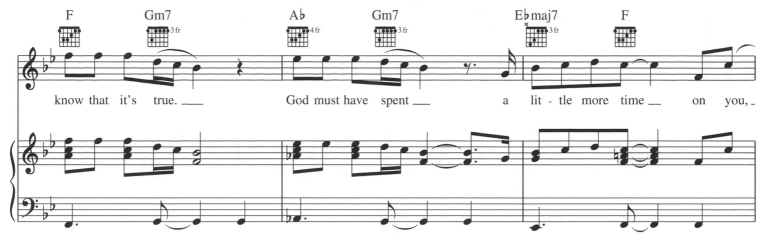

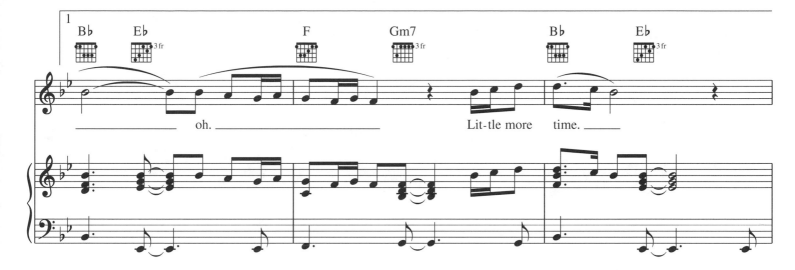

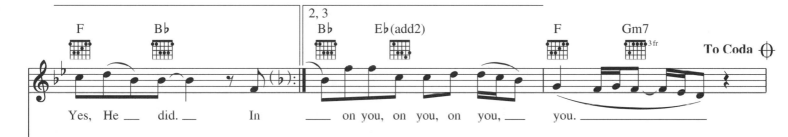

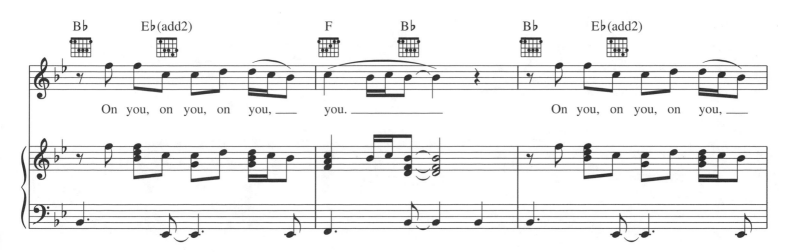

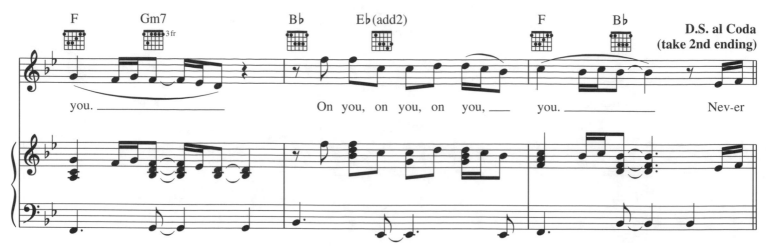

D.S. al Coda
(take 2nd ending)

you. _____ On you, on you, on you, ___ you. _____ Nev-er

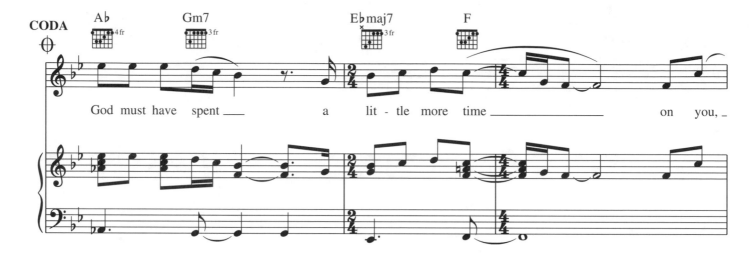

CODA

God must have spent ___ a lit-tle more time _____ on you, _

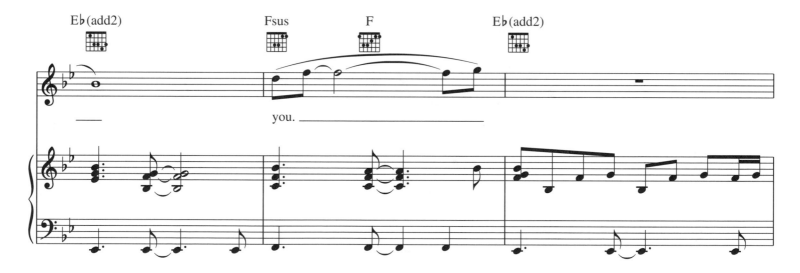

you. _____

Lit-tle more time _ on you. _____

HEARTBREAK HOTEL

Words and Music by TAMARA SAVAGE,
CARSTEN SCHACK and KENNETH KARLIN

Original Key: E♭ minor. This edition has been transposed up one half-step to be more playable.

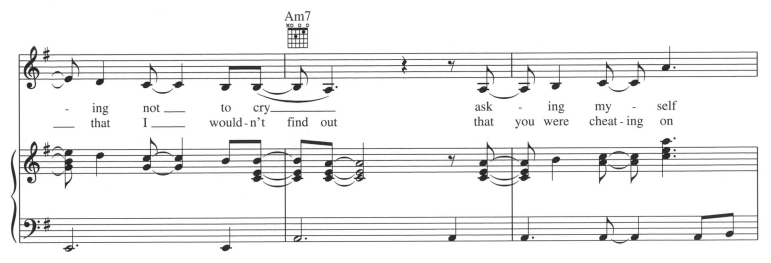

-ing not ___ to cry_____ ask - ing my - self
___ that I _____ would-n't find out that you were cheat-ing on

why _____ you do ___ this to _____ me, mmm, ___
me. _____ How___ could you do it to me?_____

ah, ba - by. __ Since you're not a - round for me to tell you, ba - by, face_

__ to face, _____ I'm writ-ing you this let - ter and

this is what __ I have __ to say: _____

All I real-ly want-ed was some of your time. __ In-stead, you told me lies when some-one else was

on your mind. __ What you do __ to me, what you do. _____ Look what you did __

__ to me, __ oh. __ ba - by. I thought that you were some-one who would

do me right __ un-til you played with my e-mo-tions and you made me cry. __ What you do __

__ to me. Can't take what you did ____ to me.

Now, I   Heart - break

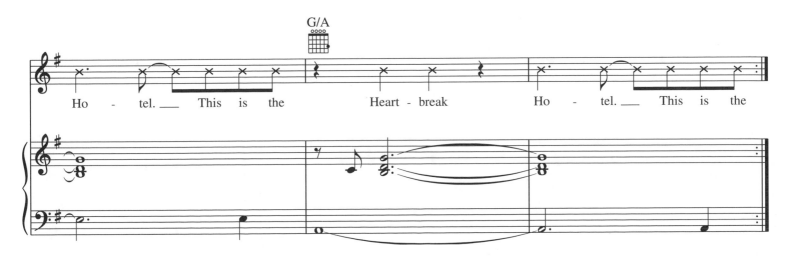

Ho - tel. __ This is the   Heart - break   Ho - tel. __ This is the

Look what you did ___ to me.

I thought that you were some-one who would do me right ___ un-til you

played with my e-mo-tions and you made me cry. ___ What you do ___ to me.

Repeat and Fade

Optional ending

Can't take what you did ___ to me.

I DON'T WANT TO WAIT

Words and Music by
PAULA COLE

Strongly

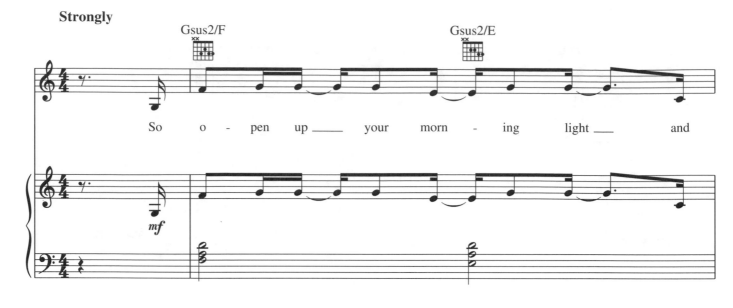

So o- pen up ____ your morn- ing light ____ and

say a lit - tle prayer ___ for I. ___ You know that if we are __ to stay __ a - live, ___ then

see the peace __ in ev - 'ry eye. ___ Du du du ___ du du,

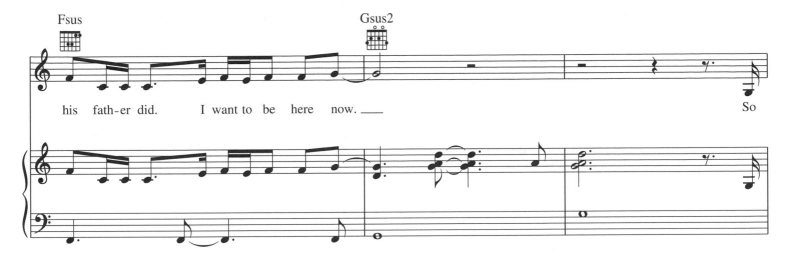

his fath-er did. I want to be here now. ___ So

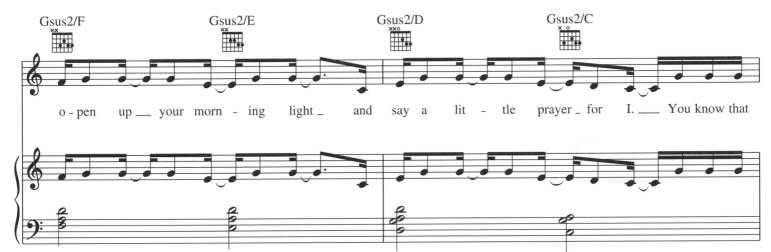

o - pen up ___ your morn - ing light _ and say a lit - tle prayer _ for I. ___ You know that

if we are ___ to stay ___ a - live, __ then see the peace _ in ev - 'ry eye. __

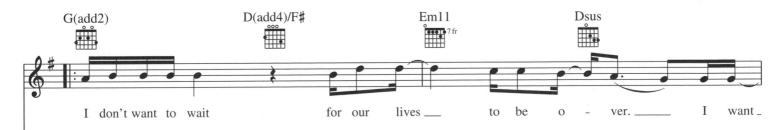

I don't want to wait for our lives ___ to be o - ver. ___ I want _

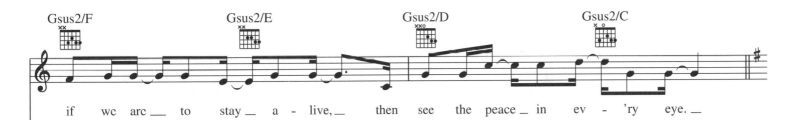

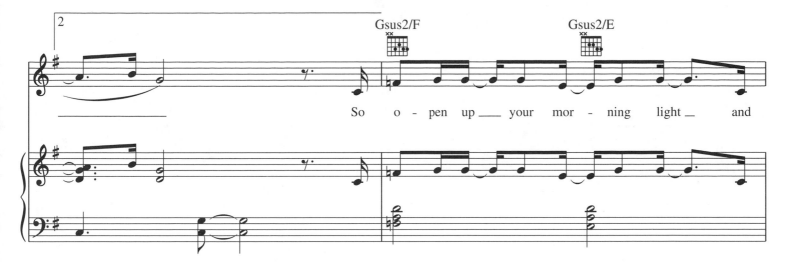

So o- pen up ___ your mor - ning light ___ and

say a lit - tle prayer ___ for I. ___ You know that if we are ___ to stay ___ a - live, ___ then

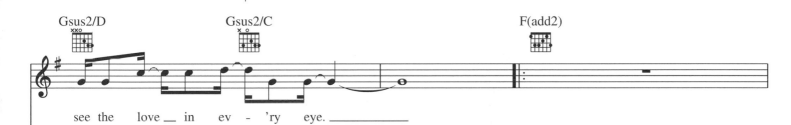

see the love ___ in ev - 'ry eye. _____

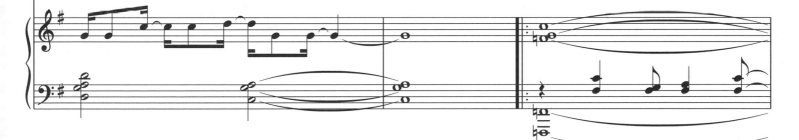

Repeat and Fade

Reprise theme of "Me"

I'LL BE

Words and Music by
EDWIN McCAIN

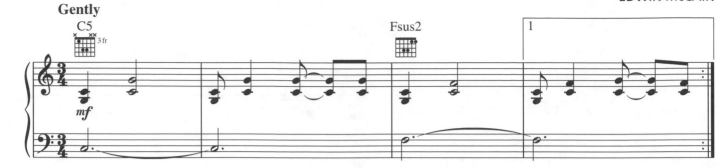

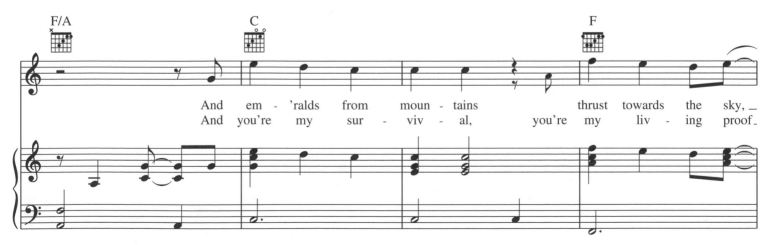

Original key: B Major. This edition has been transposed up one half-step to be more playable.

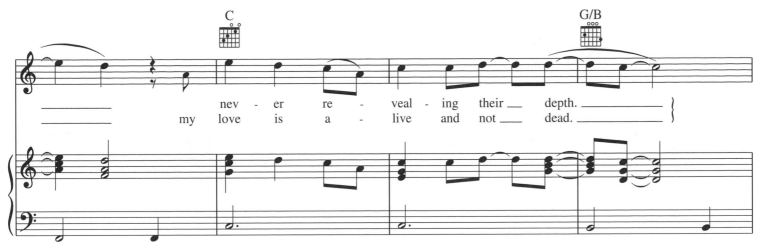

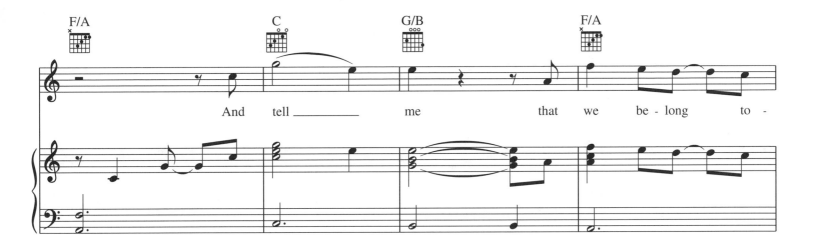

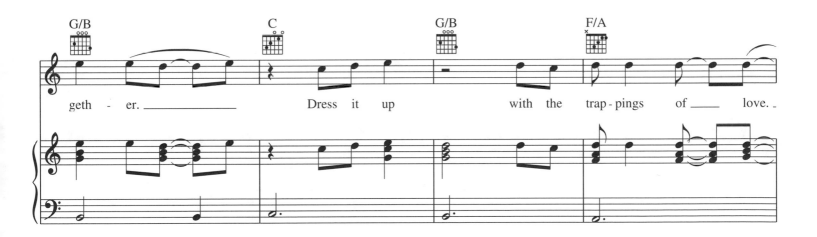

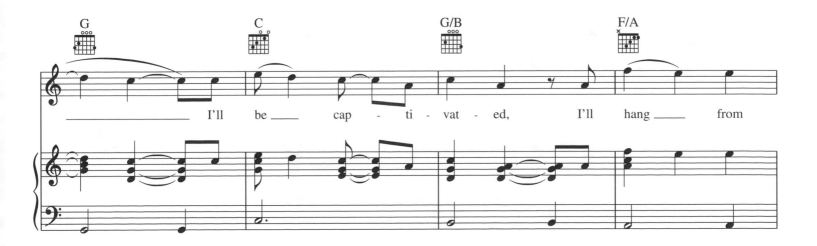

your lips in - stead of _____ the _____ gal - lows of heart - ache _____ that

hang from a - bove. _____

I'll be your cry - in' shoul - der, _____ I'll _____ be _____

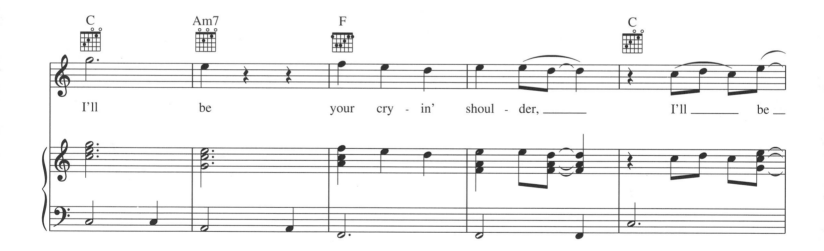

_____ love su - i - cide. _____ And I'll be

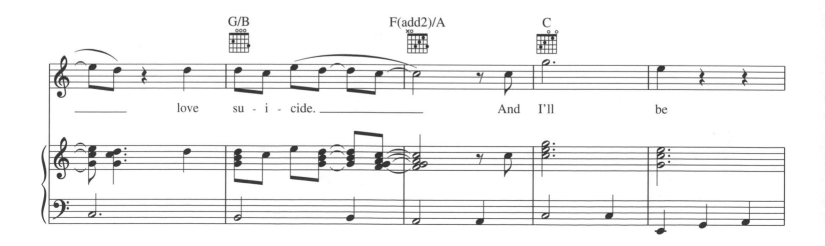

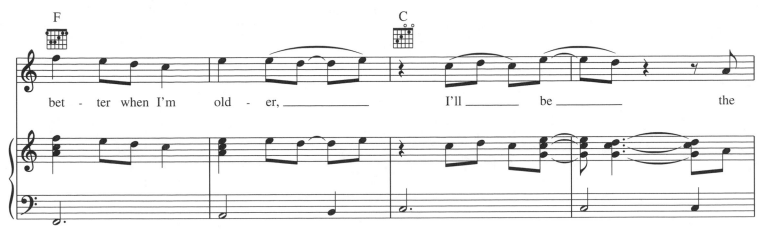

bet - ter when I'm old - er, _____ I'll ____ be ____ the

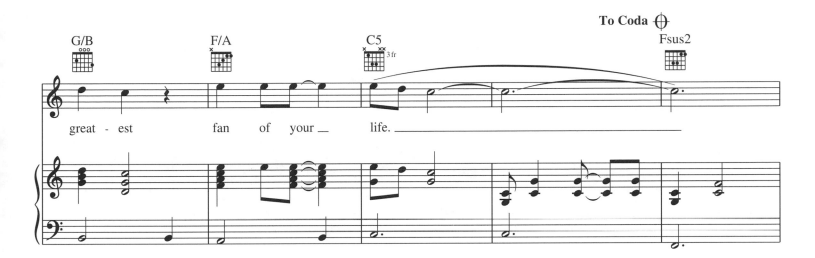

To Coda ⊕

great - est fan of your __ life. _____

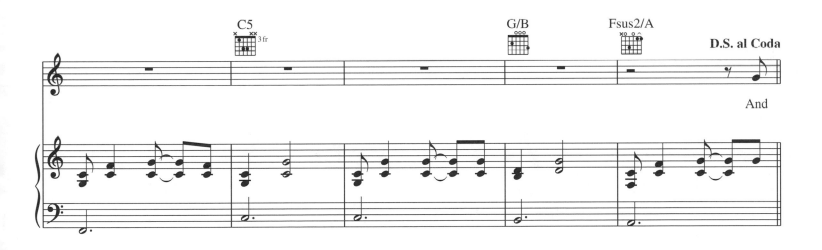

D.S. al Coda

And

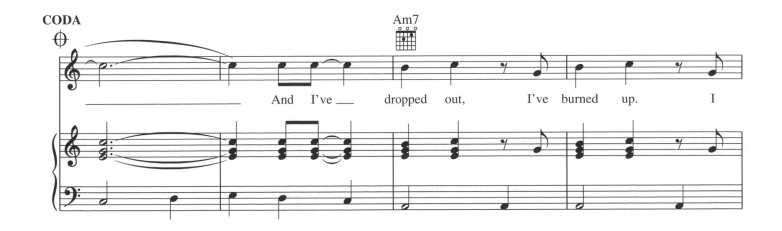

CODA ⊕

_____ And I've __ dropped out, I've burned up. I

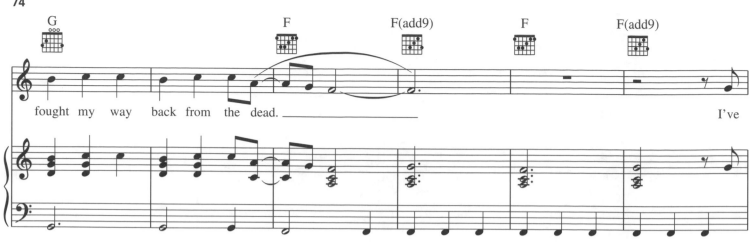

fought my way back from the dead. _____ I've

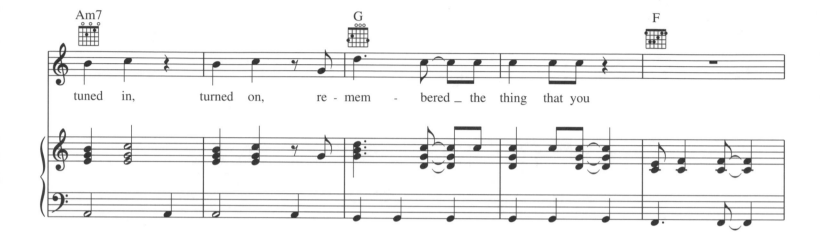

tuned in, turned on, re-mem-bered _ the thing that you

said. _____

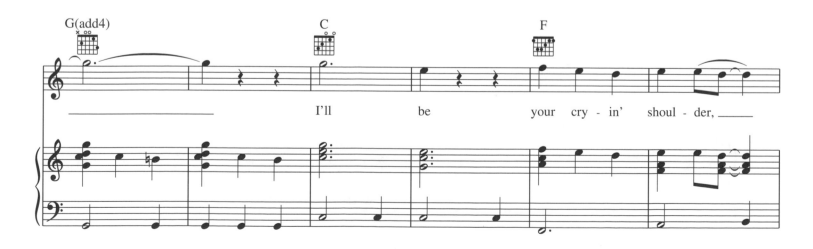

_____ I'll be your cry - in' shoul - der, _____

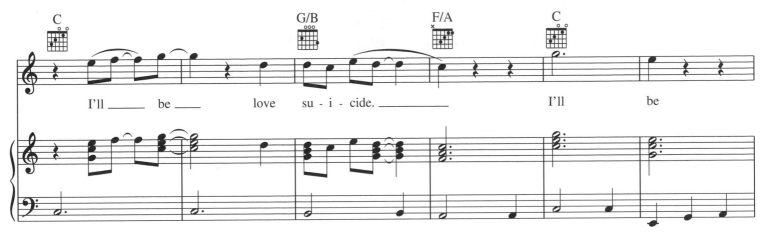

I'll ___ be ___ love su - i - cide. ___ I'll be

bet - ter when I'm old - er, ___ I'll ___ be ___ the

great - est fan of your ___ life, ___

life. ___ *Instrumental solo - ad lib.*

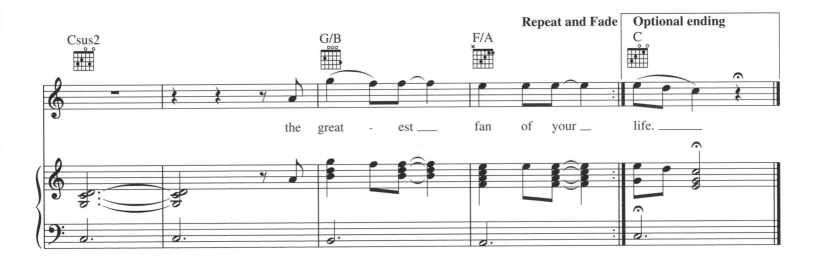

Repeat and Fade | **Optional ending**

the great - est ___ fan of your ___ life. ___

IRIS
from the Motion Picture CITY OF ANGELS

Words and Music by
JOHN RZEZNIK

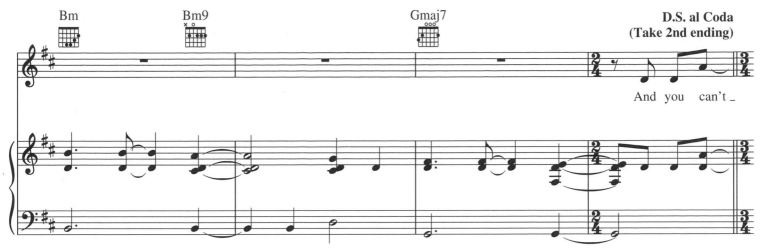

And you can't _

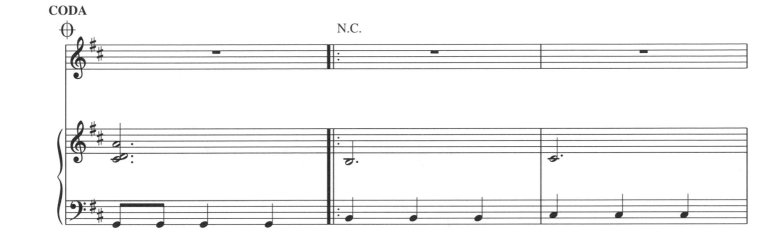

CODA

N.C.

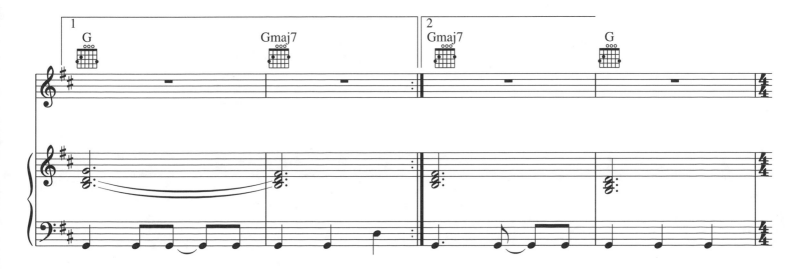

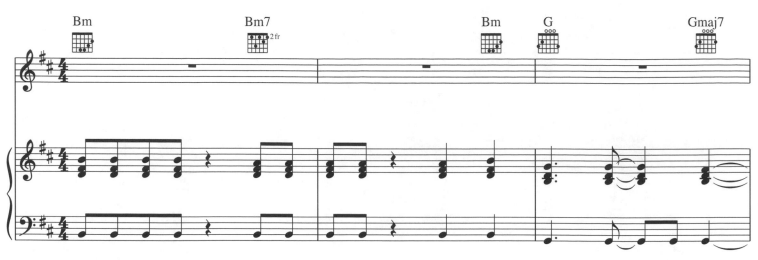

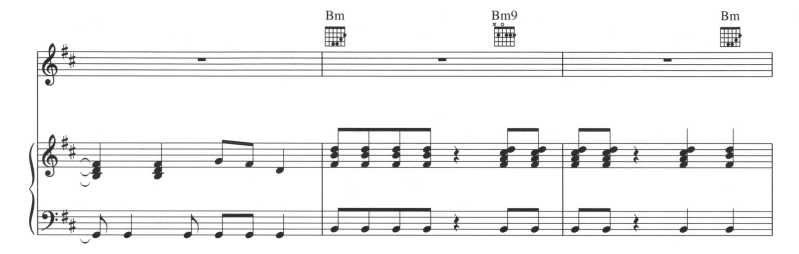

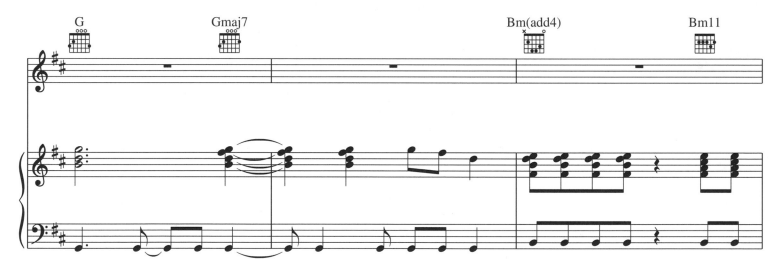

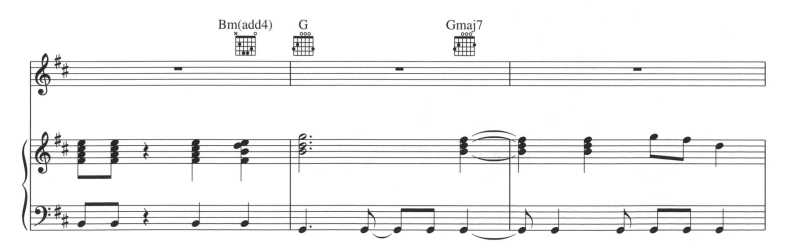

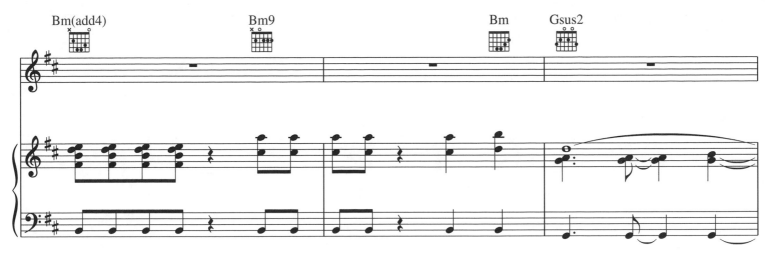

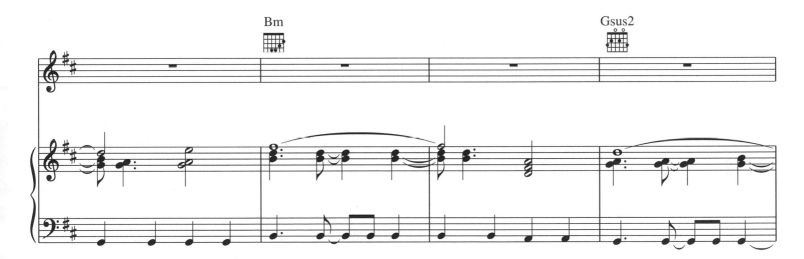

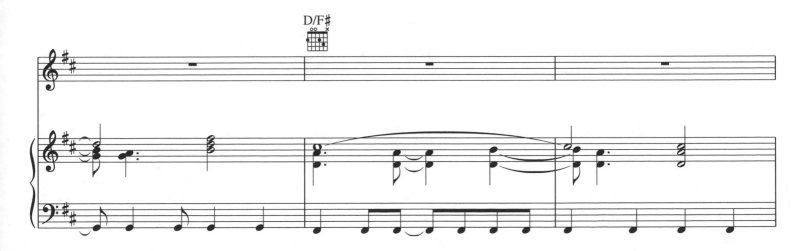

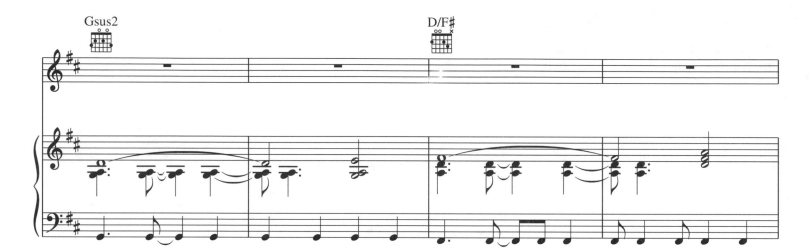

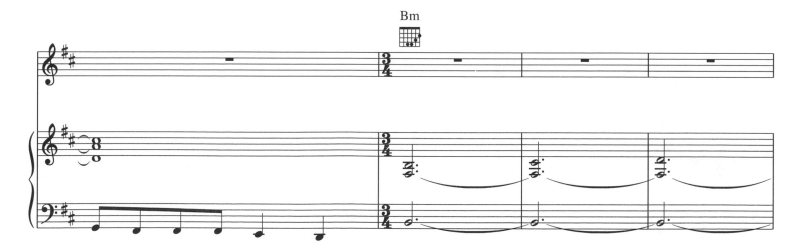

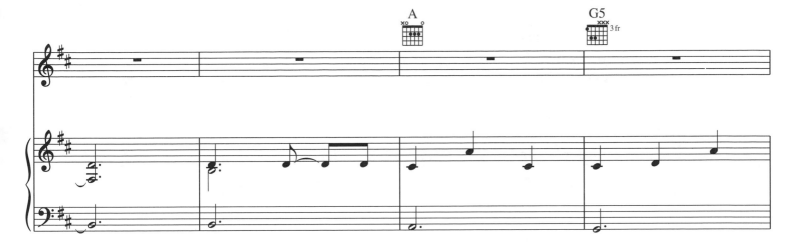

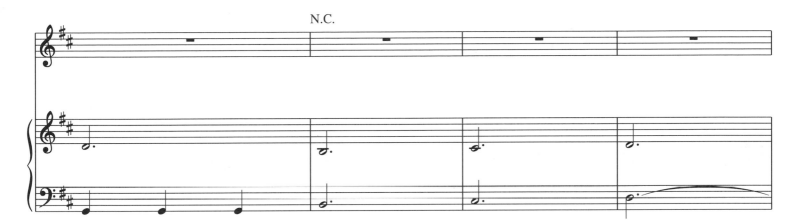

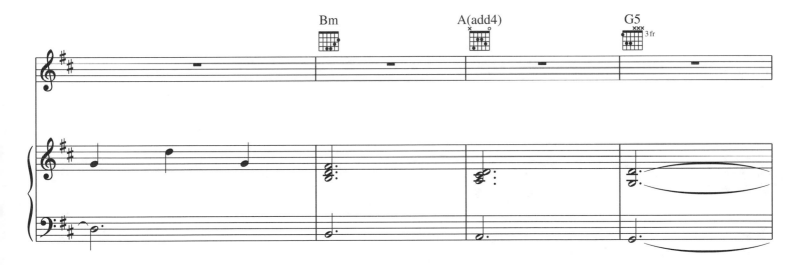

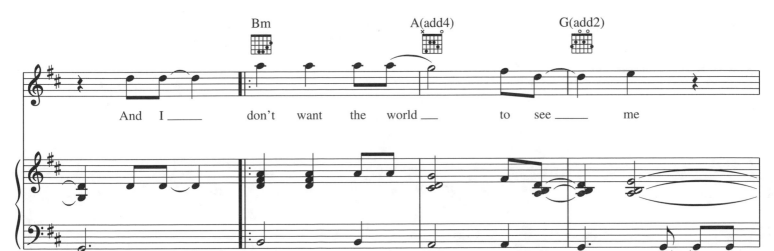

And I _____ don't want the world _____ to see _____ me

'cause I _____ don't _____ think that they'd _____ un - der - stand.

When ev - 'ry - thing's _____ made to be _____ bro - ken

I just _____ want _____ you to know _____ who I _____

am. _____ And I _____

am. I just ___ want ___ you to know ___

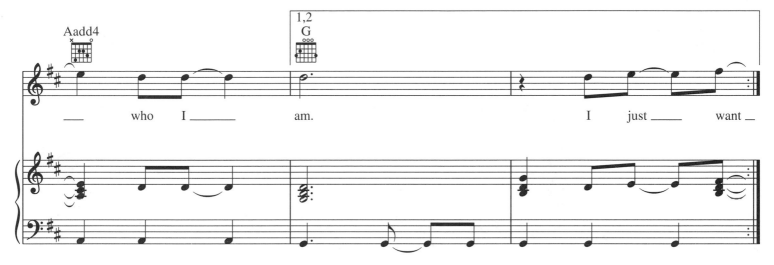

___ who I ___ am. I just ___ want ___

am. ___
Vocal 1st time only

Repeat and Fade **Optional Ending**

JUMPER

Words and Music by
STEPHAN JENKINS

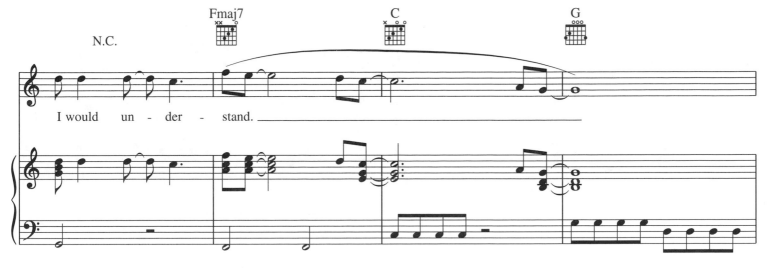

I would un - der - stand. _____

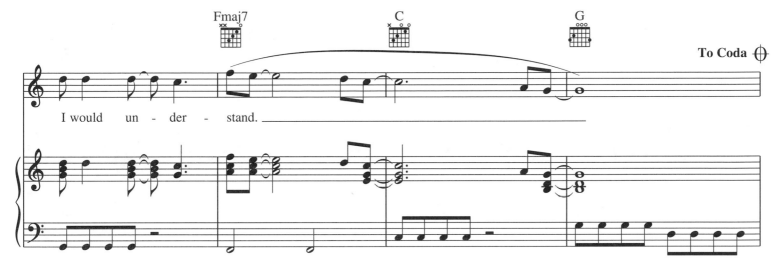

I would un - der - stand. _____

To Coda ⊕

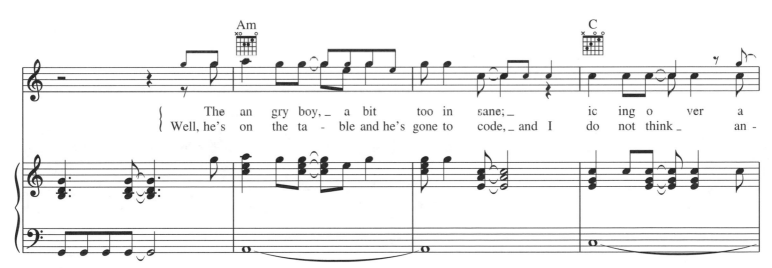

The an - gry boy, _ a bit too in - sane; _ ic - ing o - ver a
Well, he's on the ta - ble and he's gone to code, _ and I do not think _ an -

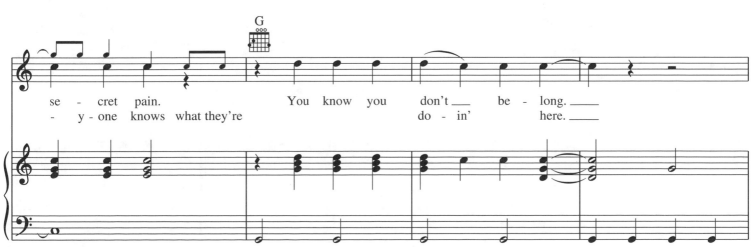

se - cret pain. You know you don't ___ be - long. ____
- y - one knows what they're do - in' here. ____

I would un - der - stand. _____

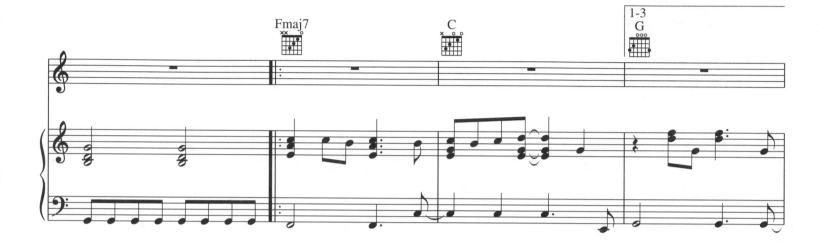

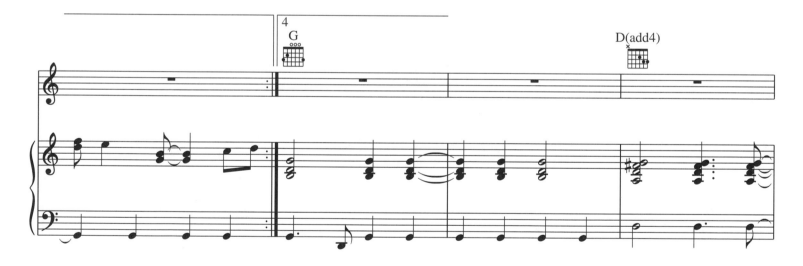

Can you put the past ___ a - way? ___ I wish you would

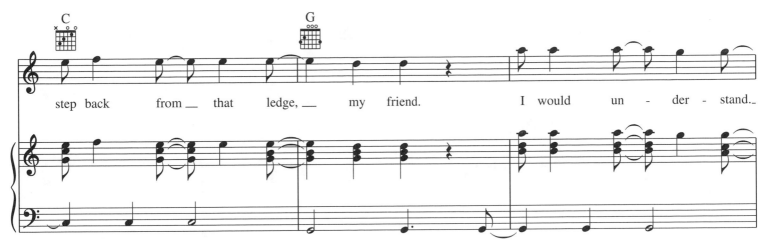

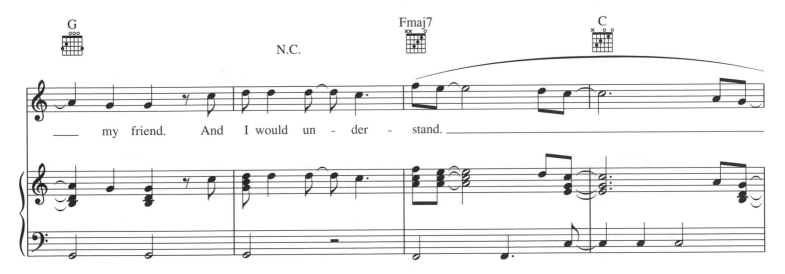

I would un - der - stand.

I would un - der - stand.

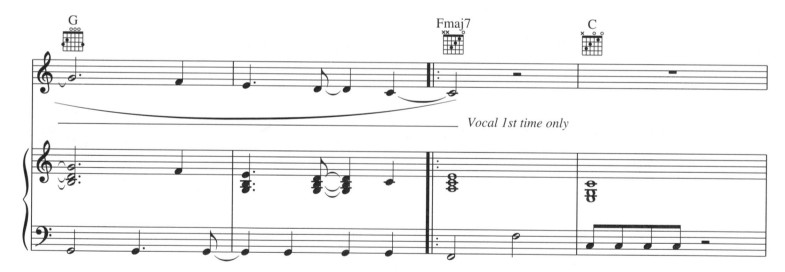

Vocal 1st time only

Play 3 times

TO LOVE YOU MORE

Words and Music by JUNIOR MILES
and DAVID FOSTER

Slowly, half-time feel

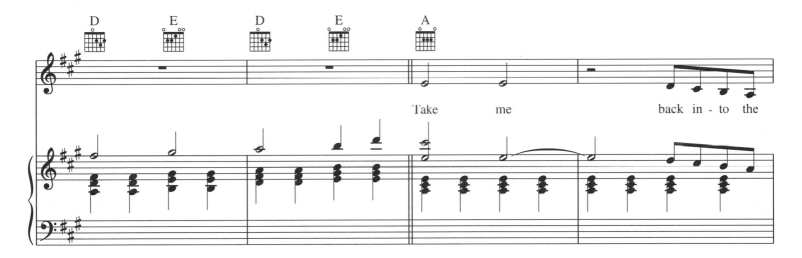

Take me back in - to the arms I love. _____ Need me like you did be - fore. _

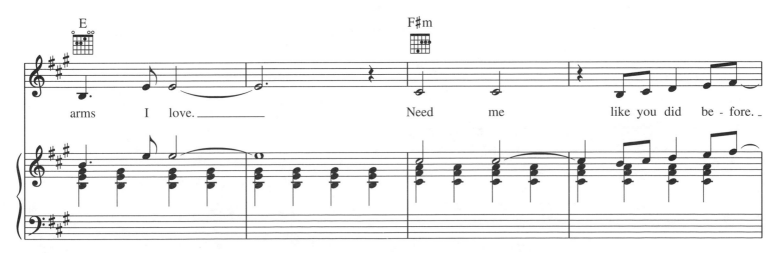

Touch me once a - gain _____ and re -

mem - ber when _____ there was no one that you want - ed

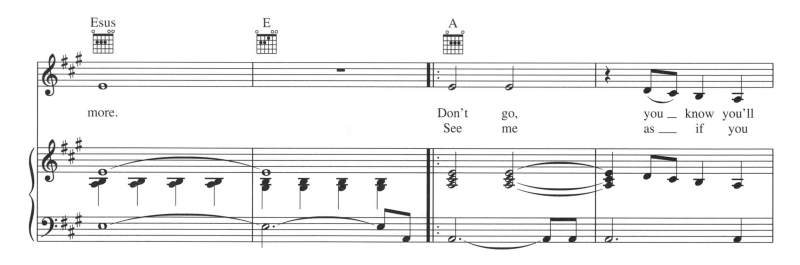

more.

Don't go, you __ know you'll
See me as __ if you

break my heart. _____
nev - er know. _____

She won't
Hold me

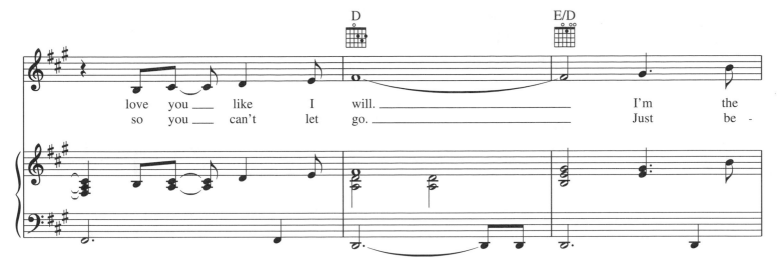

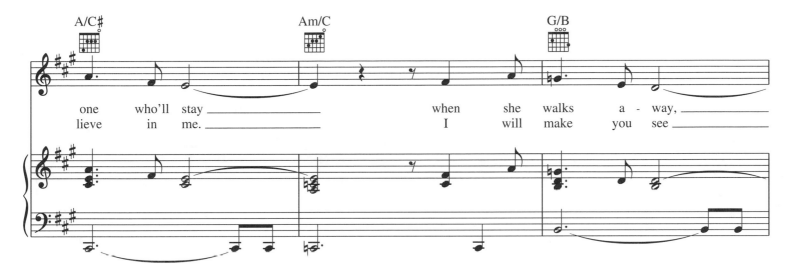

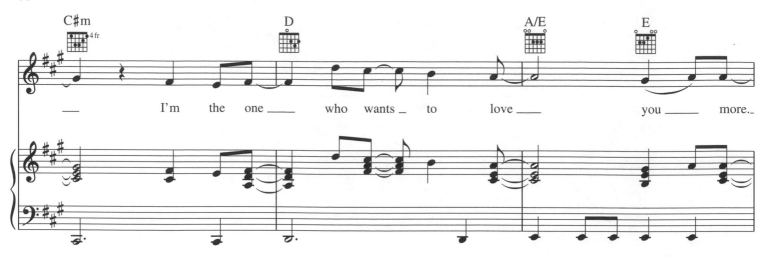

I'm the one ___ who wants ___ to love ___ you ___ more.

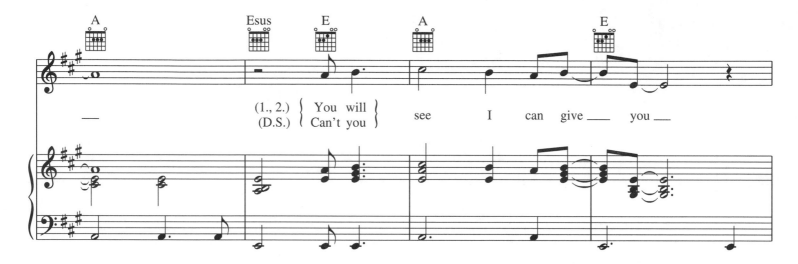

(1., 2.) { You will }
(D.S.) { Can't you } see I can give ___ you ___

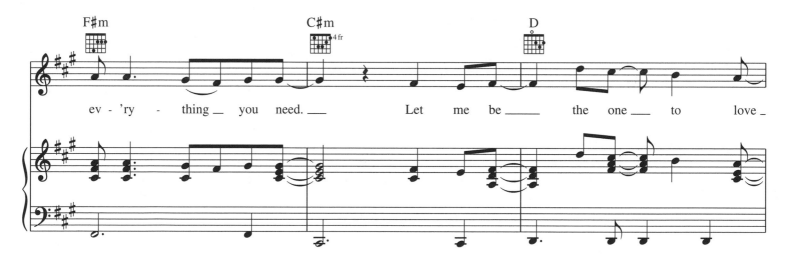

ev - 'ry - thing ___ you need. ___ Let me be ___ the one ___ to love ___

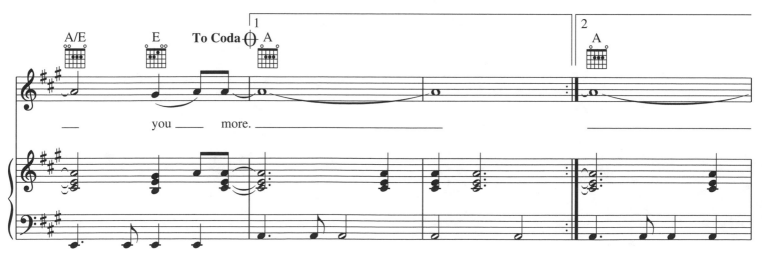

you ___ more. ___

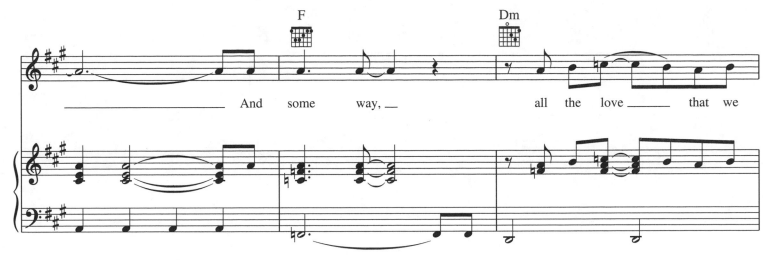

And some way, ___ all the love ___ that we

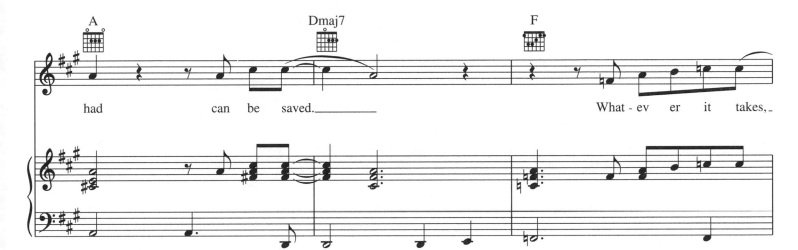

had ___ can be saved. ___ What-ev-er it takes, ___

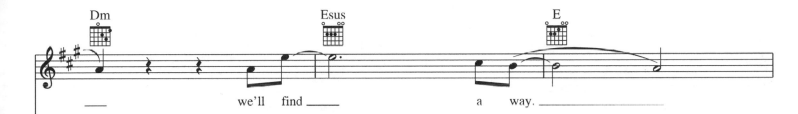

___ we'll find ___ a way. ___

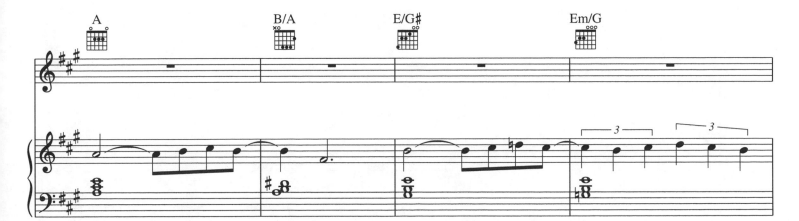

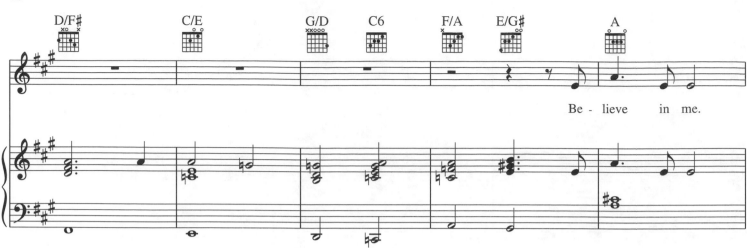

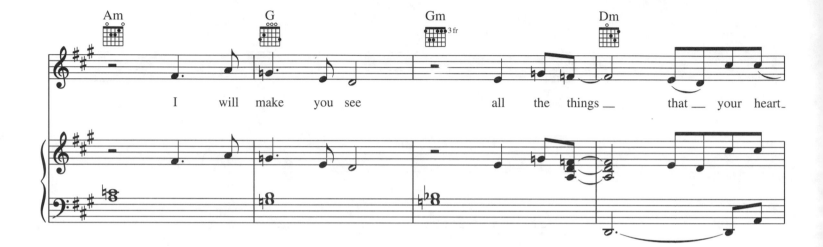

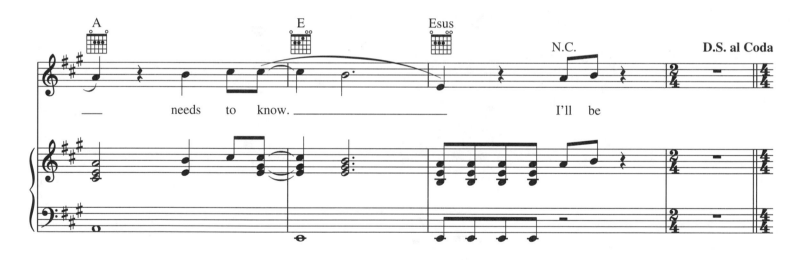

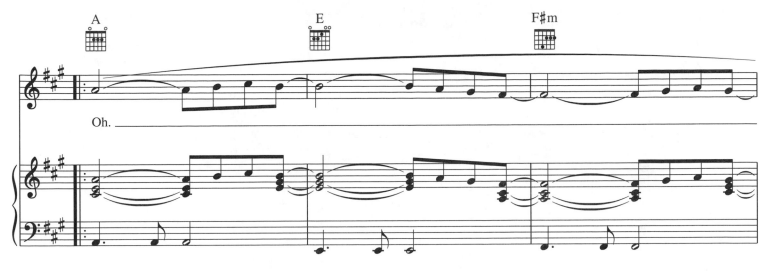

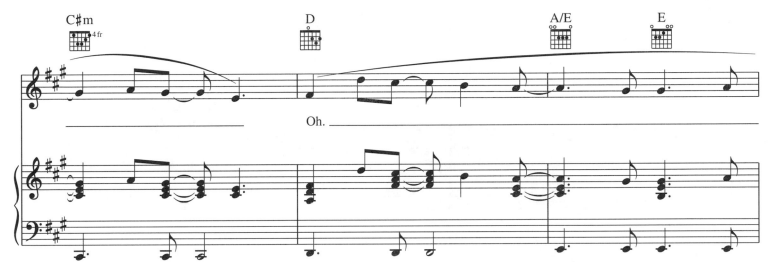

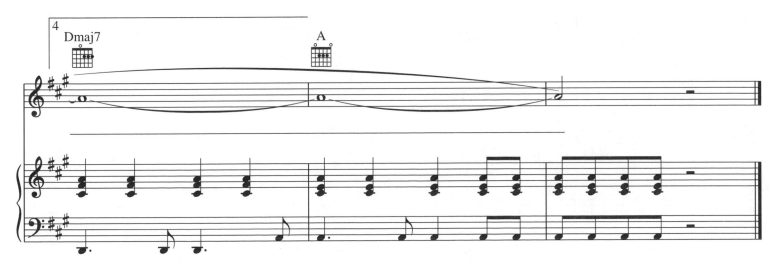

Lullaby

Words and Music by
SHAWN MULLINS

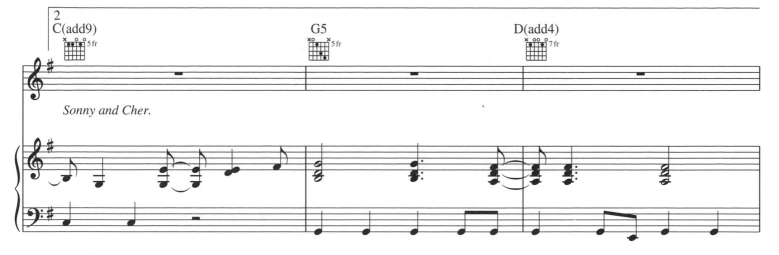

Sonny and Cher.

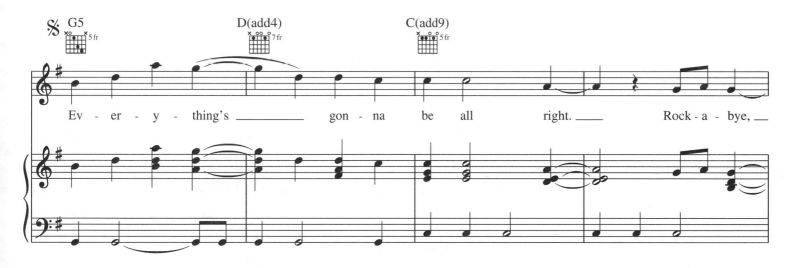

I sing:

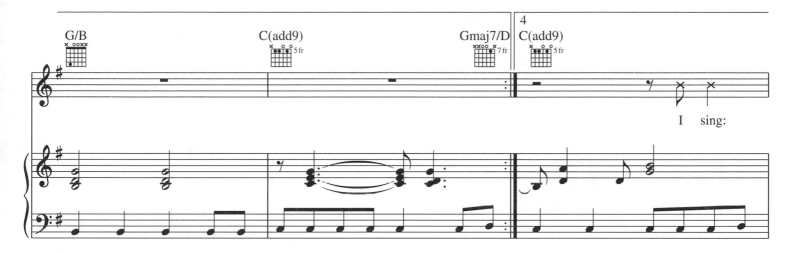

Ev - er - y - thing's _____ gon - na be all right. _____ Rock - a - bye, _____

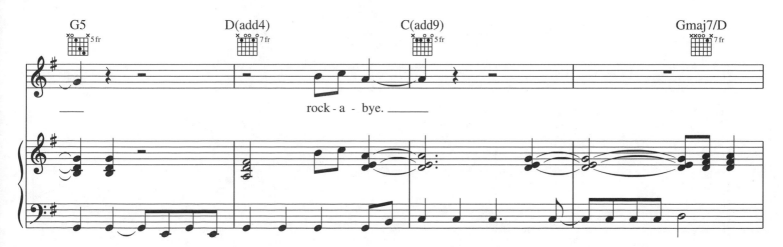

_____ rock - a - bye. _____

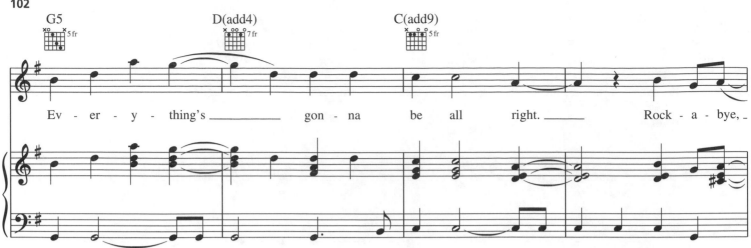

Ev - er - y - thing's _____ gon - na be all right. _____ Rock - a - bye, _

_____ rock - a - bye, ___ rock - a - bye. _

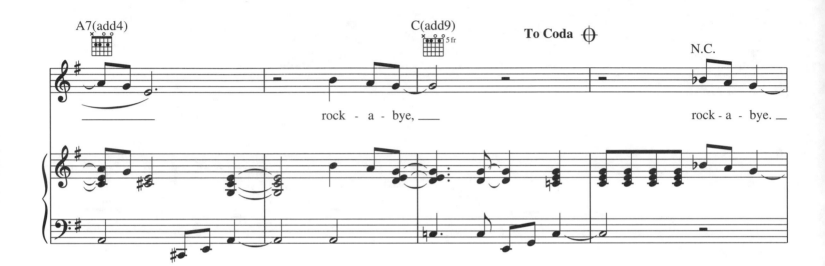

1. (Spoken:)   *She still*   *lives with her mom outside*   *the city*
2.   *And all her*   *friends tell her*   *she's so pretty,*

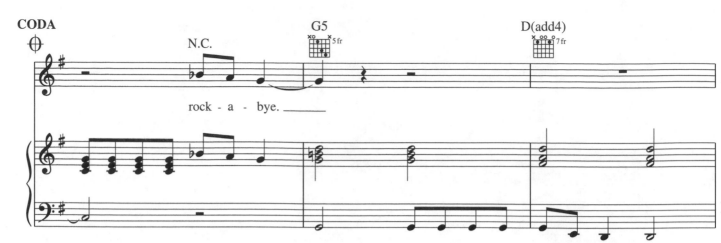

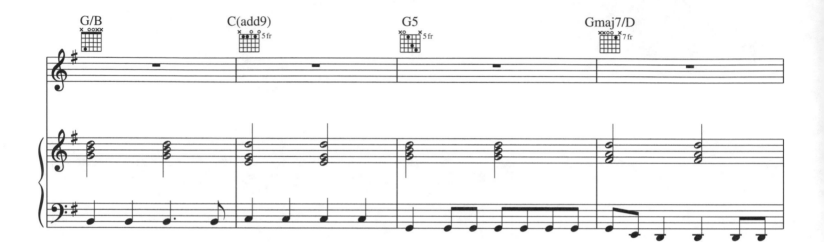

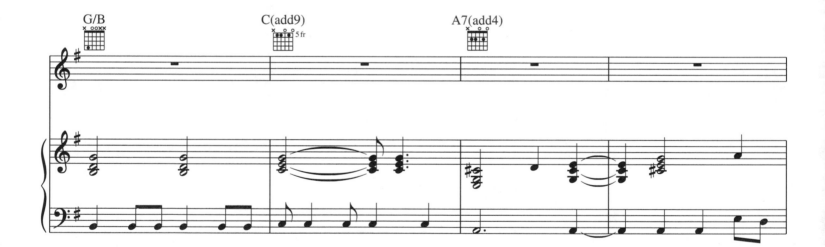

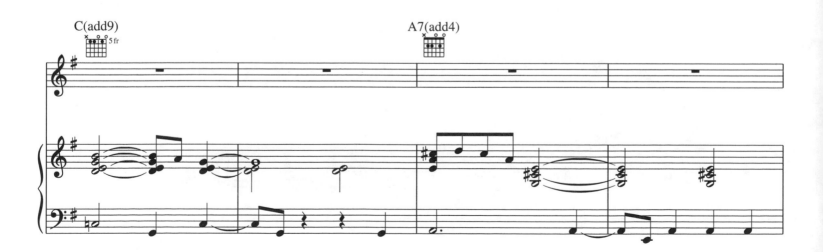

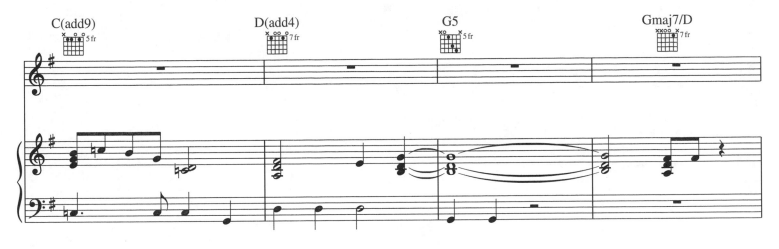

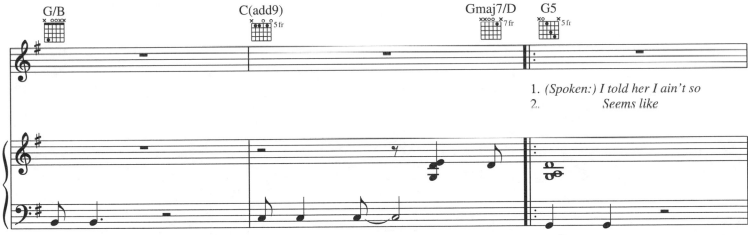

1. *(Spoken:) I told her I ain't so*
2.   *Seems like*

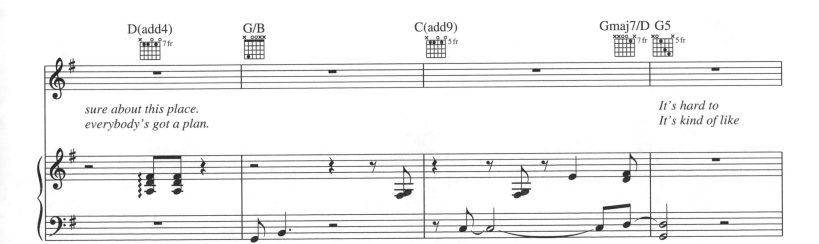

sure about this place.
everybody's got a plan.

It's hard to
It's kind of like

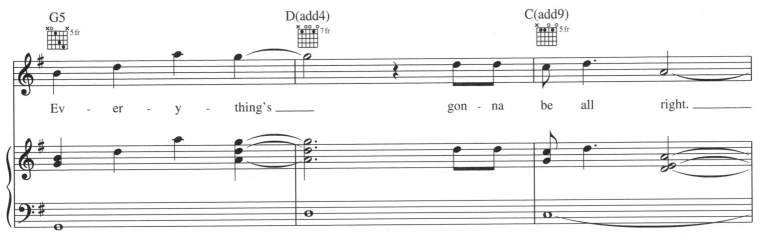

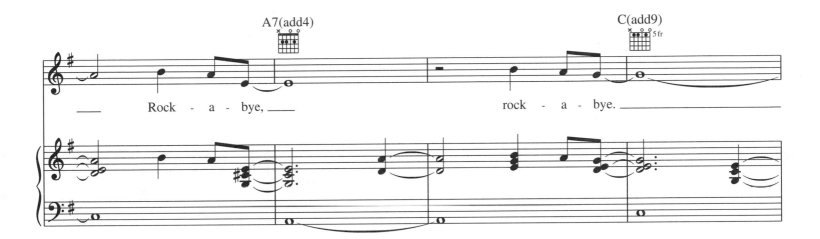

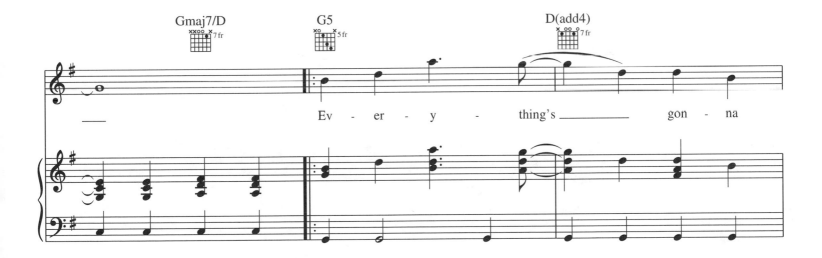

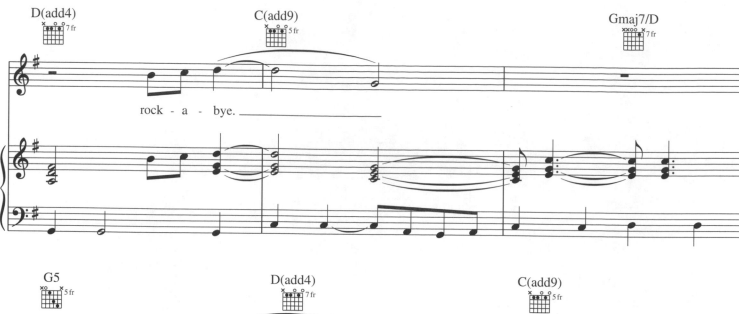

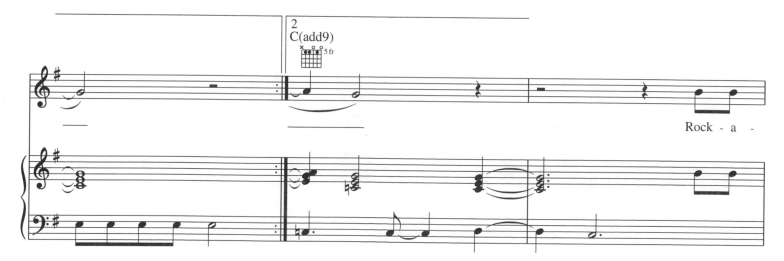

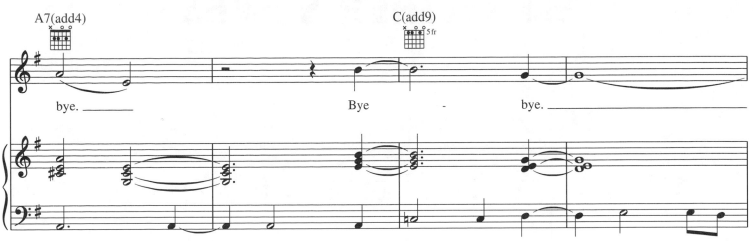

bye. _____ Bye - bye. _____

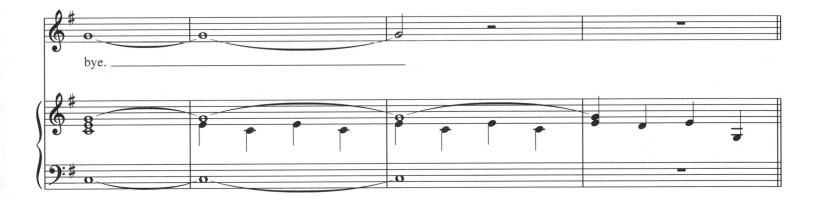

____ Bye -

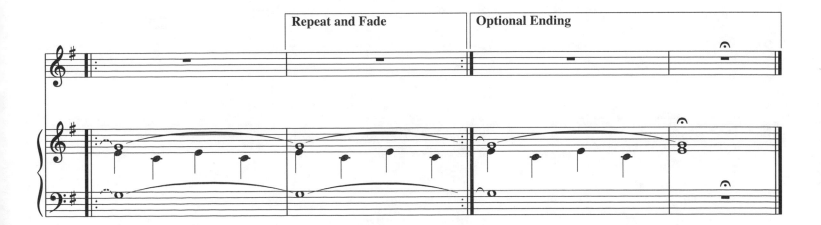

bye. _____

Repeat and Fade **Optional Ending**

MY FATHER'S EYES

Words and Music by
ERIC CLAPTON

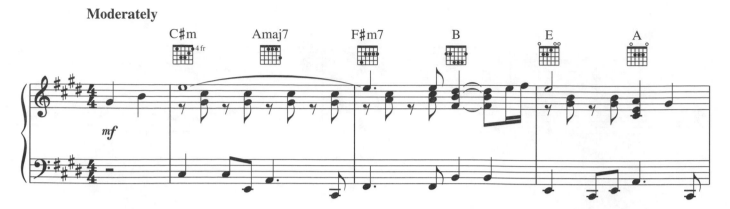

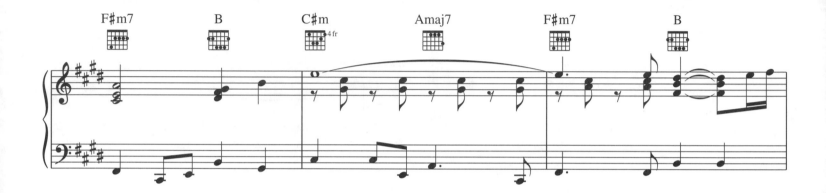

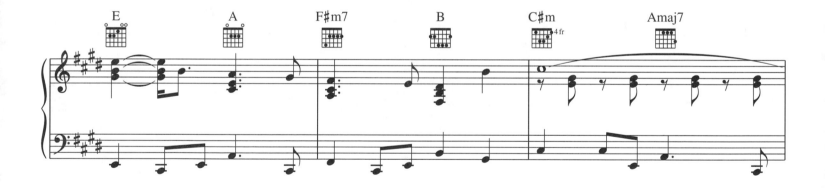

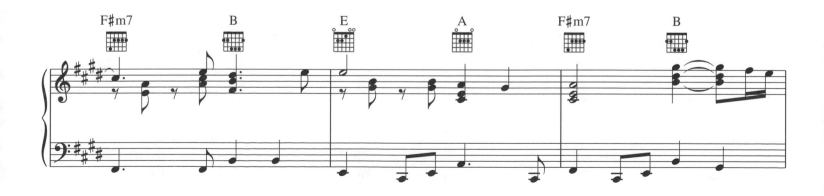

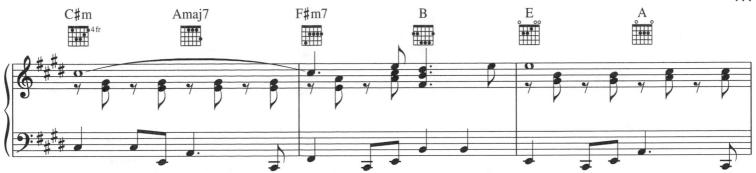

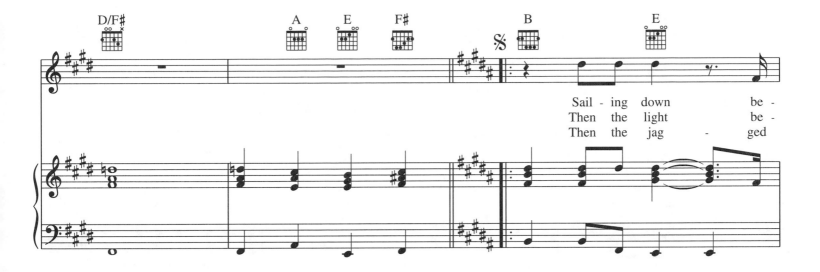

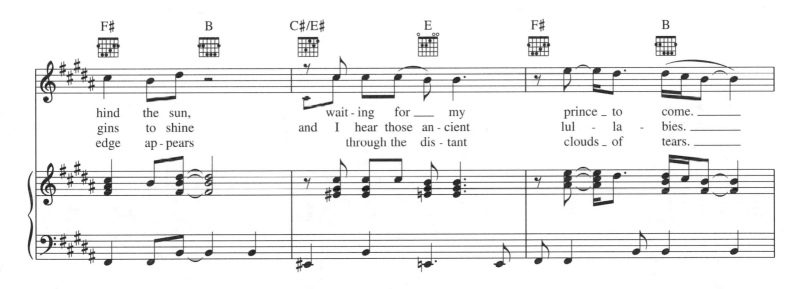

Sailing down   be-
Then the light   be-
Then the jag   -   ged

hind   the sun,   waiting for __ my
gins   to shine   and I hear those an-cient
edge ap-pears   through the dis-tant

prince __ to   come. _____
lul - la - bies. _____
clouds __ of   tears. _____

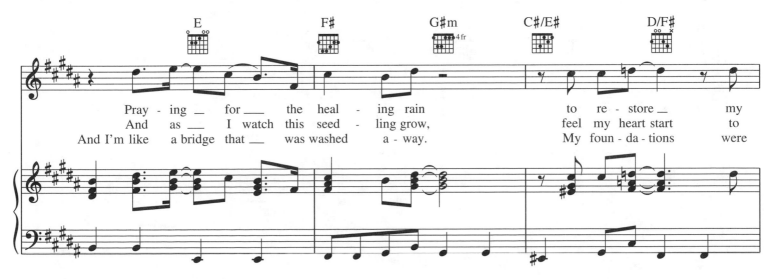

Pray-ing __ for __ the heal-ing rain   to re-store __   my
And as __ I watch this seed - ling grow,   feel my heart start to
And I'm like a bridge that __ was washed a - way.   My foun - da - tions   were

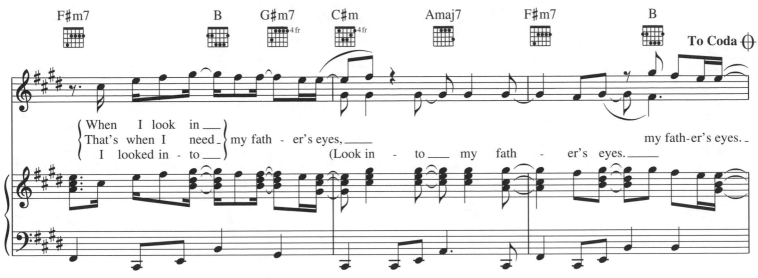

When I look in ___
That's when I need ___ } my fath - er's eyes, ___   my fath-er's eyes. ___
I looked in - to ___
(Look in - to ___ my fath - er's eyes. ___

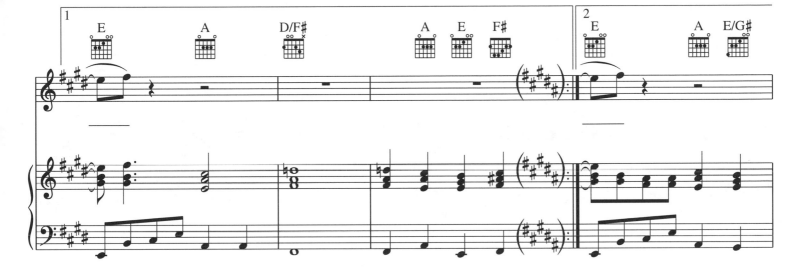

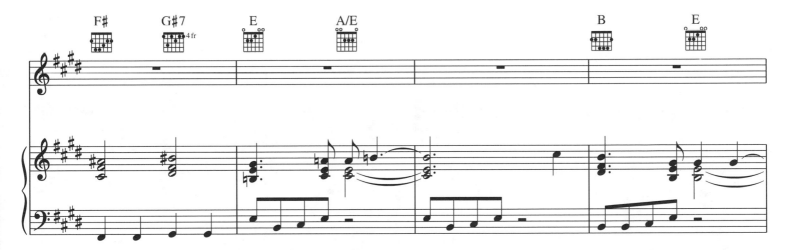

D.S. al Coda

My fath-er's eyes. __
(Looked in - to __ my fath -

MY HEART WILL GO ON
(Love Theme from 'Titanic')
from the Paramount and Twentieth Century Fox Motion Picture TITANIC

Music by JAMES HORNER
Lyric by WILL JENNINGS

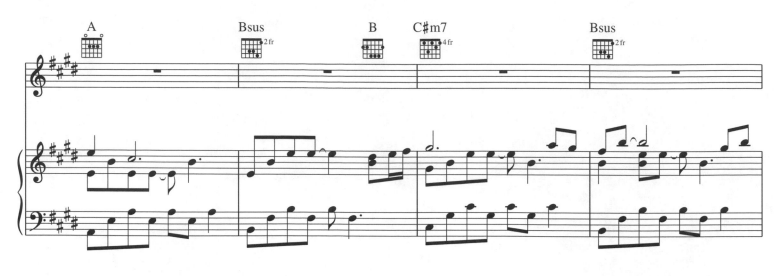

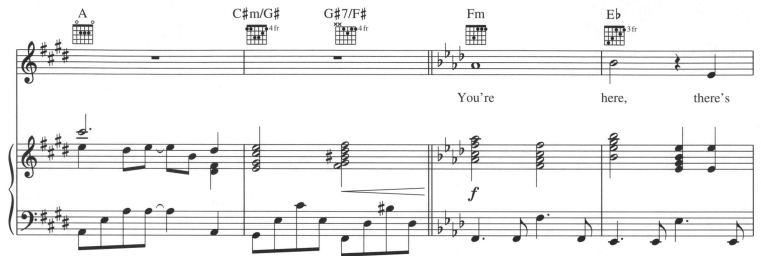

You're here, there's

noth - ing I fear ___ and I know ___ that my heart will go

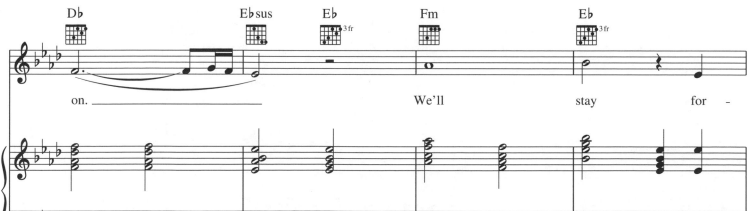

on. _____ We'll stay for -

NOBODY'S SUPPOSED TO BE HERE

Words and Music by MONTELL JORDAN
and ANTHONY "SHEP" CRAWFORD

take some time __ and take care of me, ___ but I turn a - round __ and

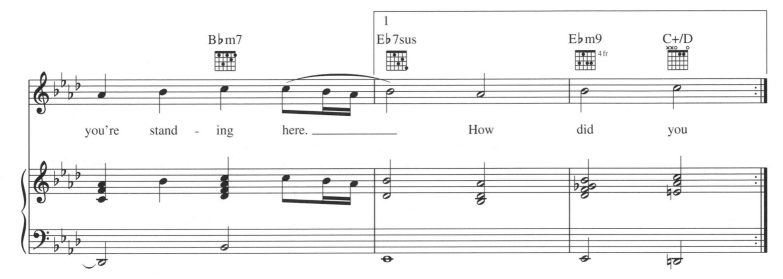

you're stand - ing here. _____ How did you

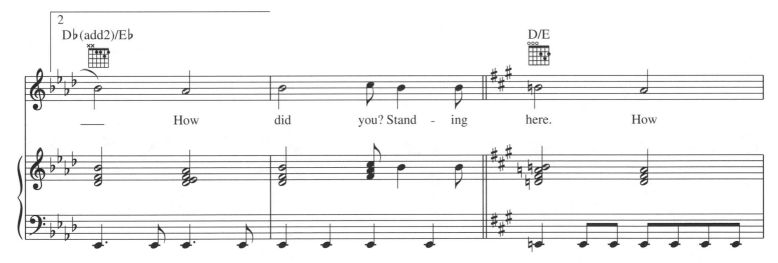

___ How did you? Stand - ing here. How

did you get here? No - no - bod - y, shoo bee doo, no - bod - y's s'posed to

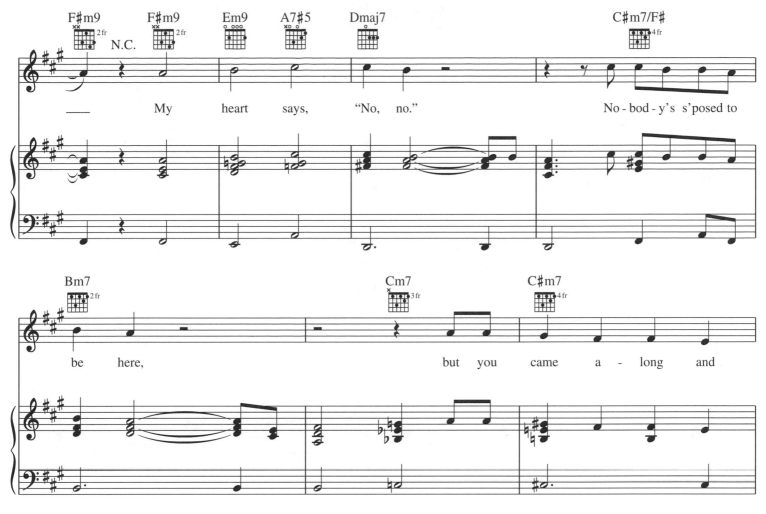

My heart says, "No, no." No - bod - y's s'posed to

be here, but you came a - long and

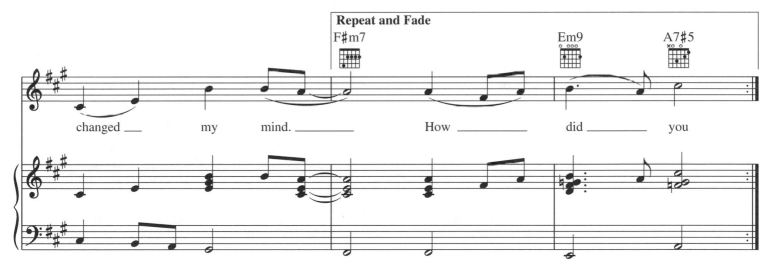

changed ___ my mind. _____ How _____ did _____ you

Repeat and Fade

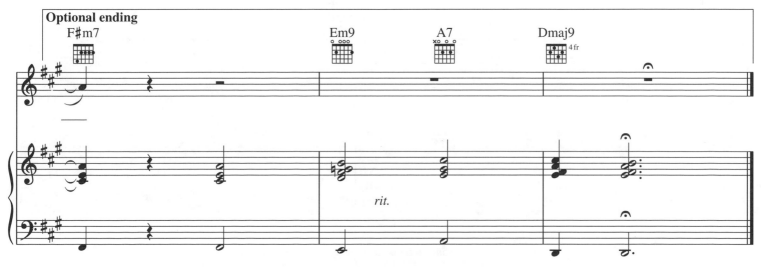

Optional ending

rit.

SLIDE

Words and Music by
JOHN RZEZNIK

Yeah, _____ we're gon-na let it slide._

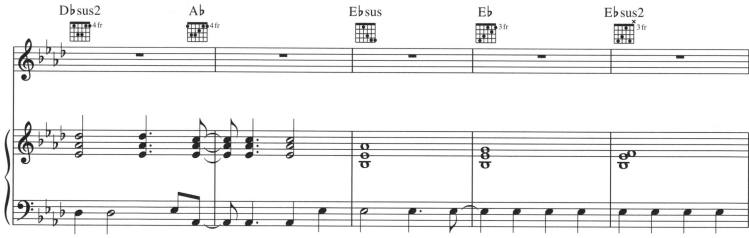

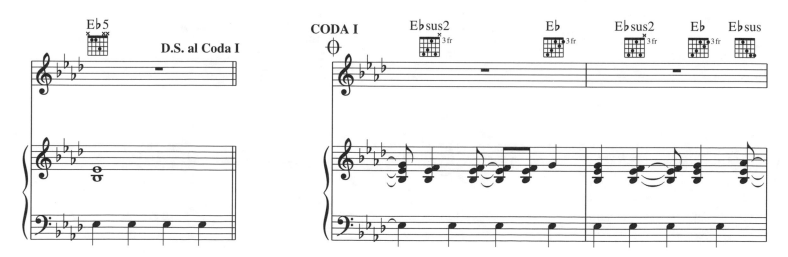

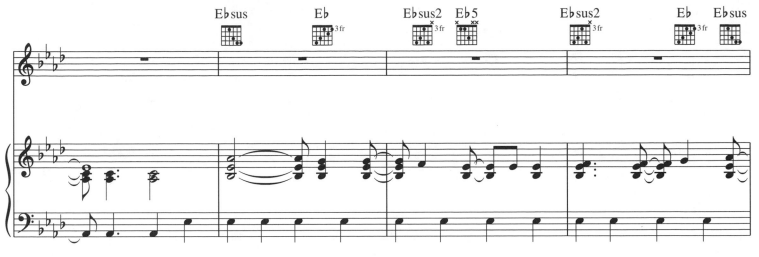

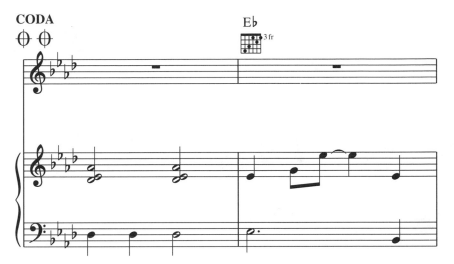

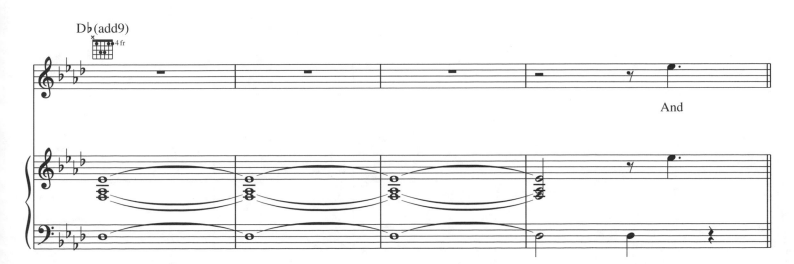

I'll do an-y-thing ___ you ev - er dream to be ___ com - plete.

Lit - tle piec - es of the noth - ing that fall. ___

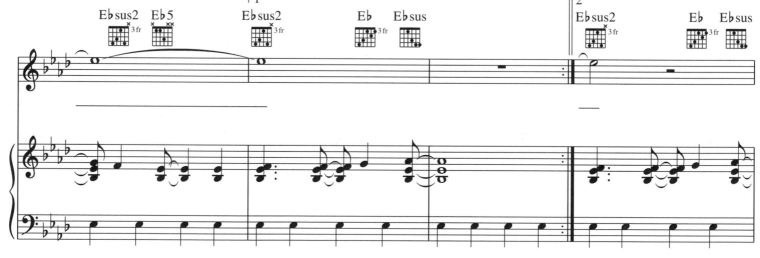

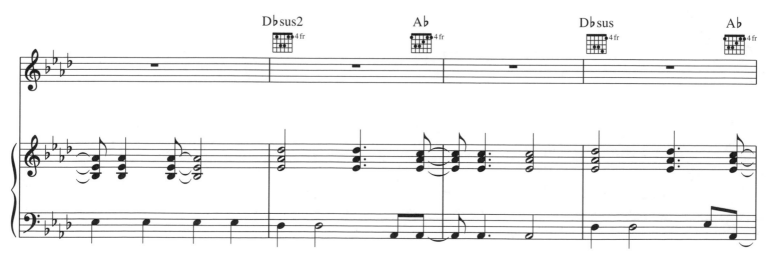

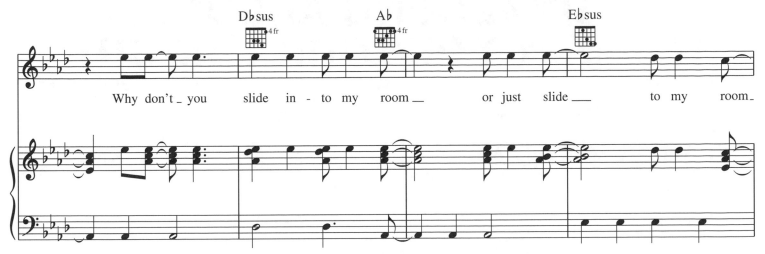

Why don't _ you slide in - to my room _ or just slide _ to my room _

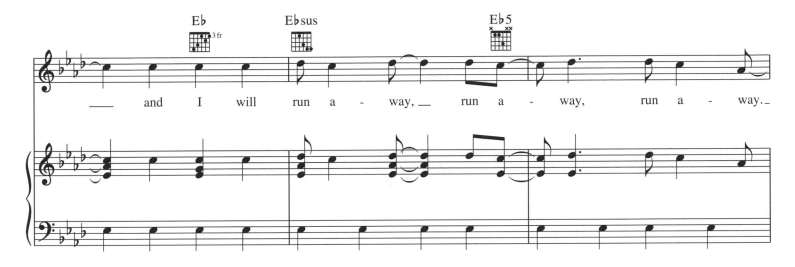

_ and I will run a - way, _ run a - way, run a - way. _

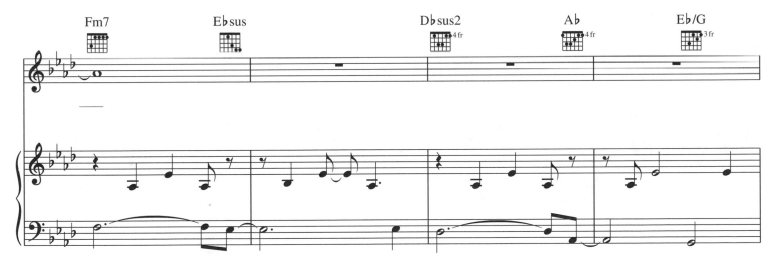

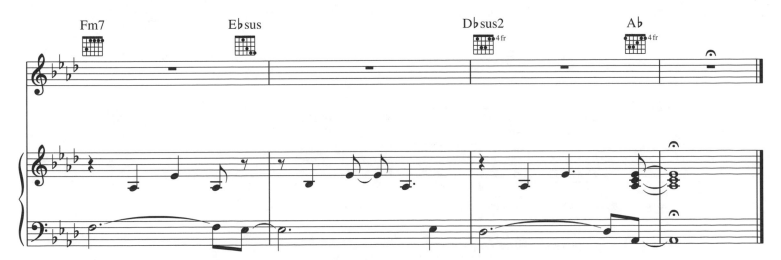

SOMETHING ABOUT THE WAY YOU LOOK TONIGHT

Words and Music by ELTON JOHN
and BERNIE TAUPIN

Original Key: F-sharp major. This edition has been transposed down one half-step to be more playable.

I was feel-ing like ___ a cloud ___ a-cross the sun. ___
you just shine like ___ a bea - con of the bay. ___
I'm speech-less and ___ I don't know where to start. ___

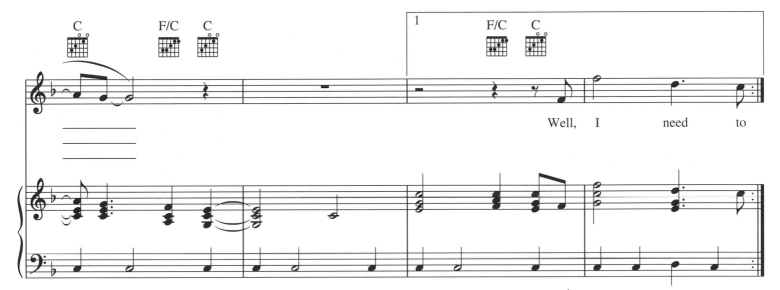

Well, I need to

And I can't ex - plain, ___

but there's some-thing a-bout ___ the way ___ you

but there's some-thing a-bout ___ the way ___ you look to-night, ___ takes my breath a-way. _____

The way you look ___ to-night.

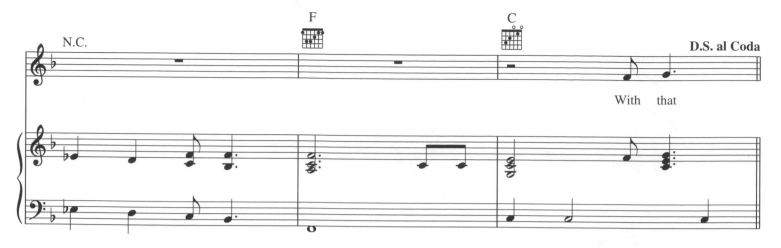

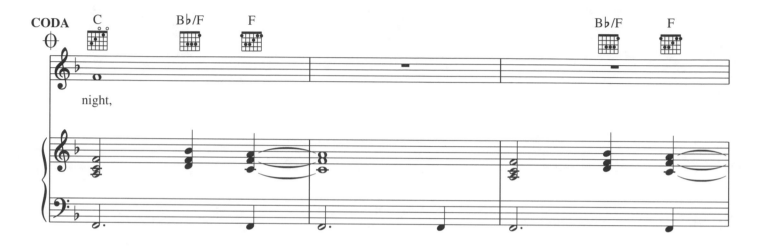

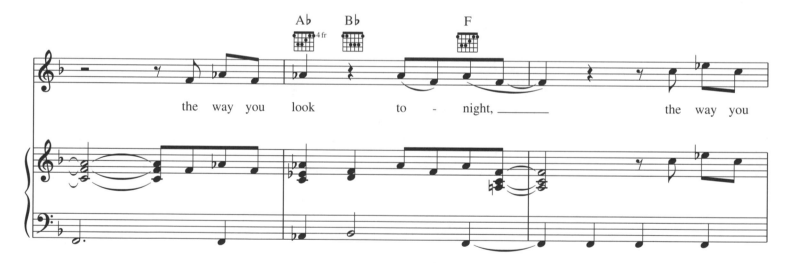

the way you look to - night, _____ the way you

look to - night, _____ the way you look to - night, _

the way you look to - night, _____ the way you

look _____ to - night. _____

TAKE ME THERE

Words and Music by TEDDY RILEY,
TAMARA SAVAGE, MASON BETHA, MICHAEL FOSTER,
MADELINE NELSON and MARK MOTHERSBAUGH

Bdim
E7(no3rd)
Am
a - bout what we did and how we used to play.
'cause you know that ev - 'ry - thing will be al - right.
Fmaj7
N.C.
G9sus
3fr
Am
Just the thought of you brings a smile up - on my face.
I see the mag - ic in your eyes.
Bm7♭5
B7(add13)
Am
It's how it makes me feel to see you ev - e - ry day. Whoa.
It's strong e - nough, you know, to bring your dreams to life. Oh.
Fmaj7
G
Am
(Female:)
Oh, where we go, no - bod - y knows

Additional Lyrics

Rap: Angelica the one with all exposure,
Dil is the one they drop in the stroller.
And Tommy got the whole world on his shoulder,
'Cause Dil cried to sleep till his eyes looked beat.
And I couldn't have been Chucky, Chucky too petro.
Chucky gets scared. Chucky said, "Let's go."
If I was a Rugrat, it would have been so real.
Me and my twin would have been just like Phil and Lil.

And with one wish, blink, grant you one trip.
Where we goin' this adventure? Who you wanna come with?
See, you're my little brother that I'll come get, run wit.
But it got to be done quick.
Though Chucky is scared and Tommy is sad
And Phil and Lil misses their mommy and dad.
So pick a time and date and find a place,
And I guarantee you that we all get home safe.

THANK U

Words by ALANIS MORISSETTE
Music by ALANIS MORISSETTE
and GLEN BALLARD

150

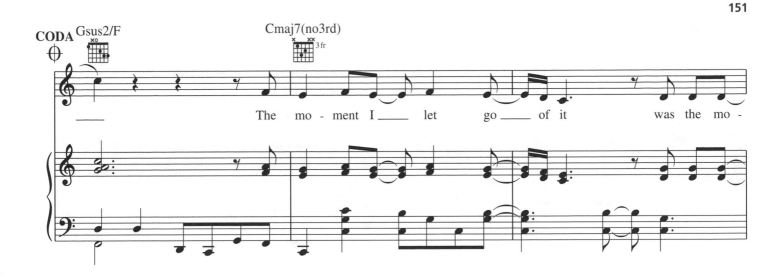

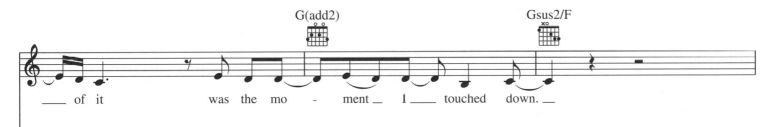

How 'bout re-mem-ber-ing ____ your di-vin-i-ty.

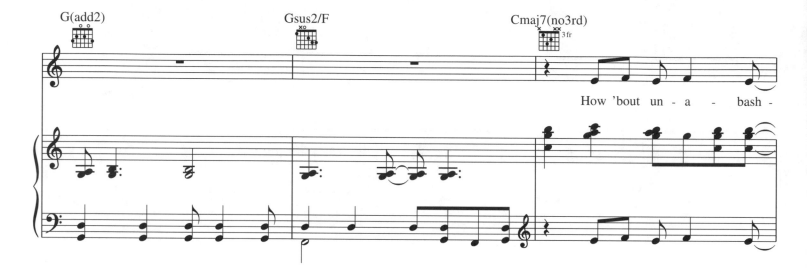

How 'bout un-a-bash-

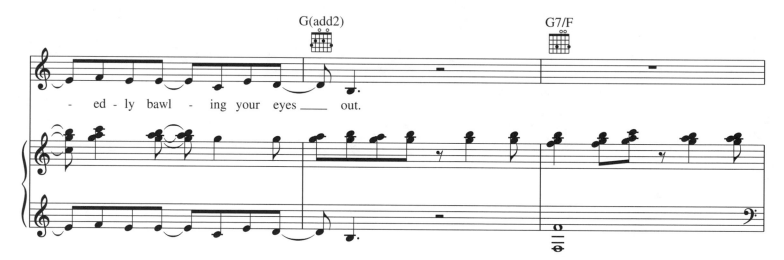

-ed-ly bawl-ing your eyes ____ out.

How 'bout not e-quat-ing ____ death with ____ stop-ping. ____

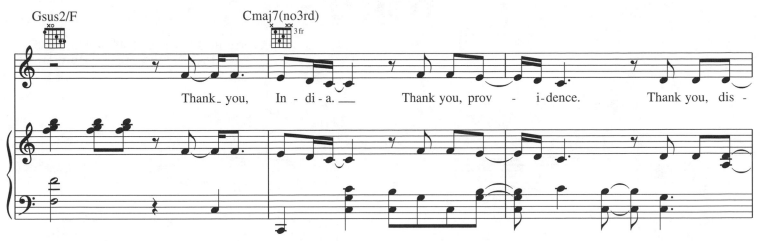

Thank_ you, In - di - a. __ Thank you, prov - i - dence. Thank you, dis -

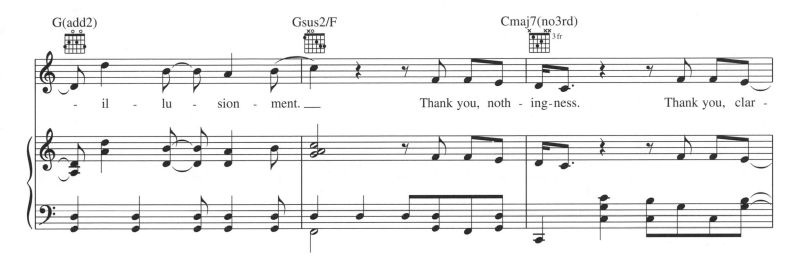

- il - lu - sion - ment. __ Thank you, noth - ing - ness. Thank you, clar -

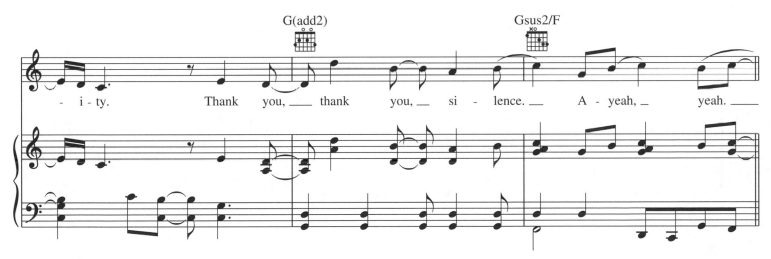

- i - ty. Thank you, __ thank you, __ si - lence. __ A - yeah, __ yeah. __

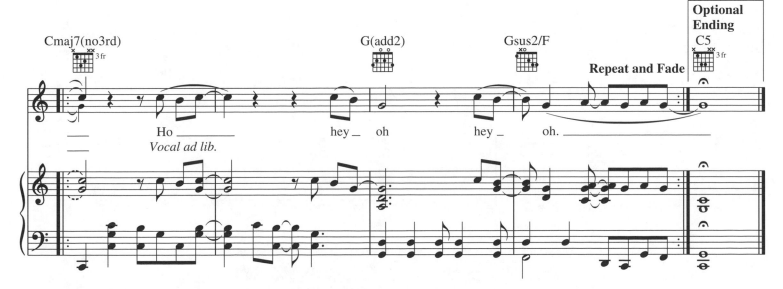

Ho __ hey_ oh hey_ oh. __

Vocal ad lib.

Optional Ending

Repeat and Fade

TORN

Words and Music by PHIL THORNALLEY,
ANNE PREVIN and SCOTT CUTLER

Moderate Rock

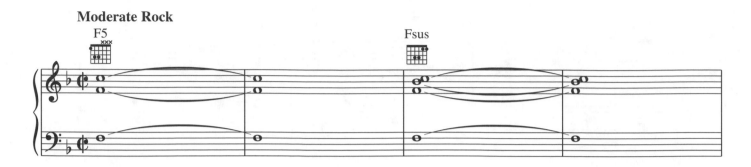

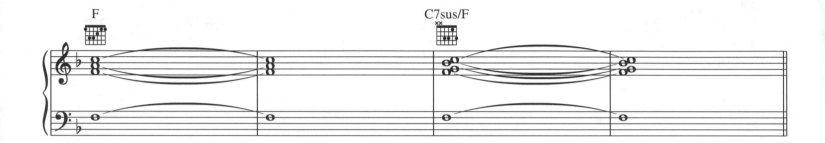

I thought I saw ___ a man ___ brought ___
Well, you could-n't be ___ that man ___ I ___
So, I guess ___ the for-tune tell-

___ to life. ___ He was warm, ___
___ a - dored. ___ You don't seem to know ___
-er's right. ___ I should-'ve seen ___

he came a - round ___ like he was dig - ni - fied. ___
or seem to care ___ what your heart ___ is for. ___
just what was there ___ and not some hol - y light. ___

He showed me what it was ___ to cry.
Well, I don't know him an -
But you crawled be - neath my veins ___

- y - more. There's noth - ing where ___ he used to lie. ___
___ and now I don't care, ___ I have no luck. ___

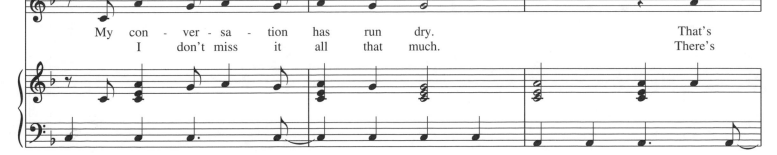

My con - ver - sa - tion has run dry.
I don't miss it all that much. That's
There's

whats go - ing on. _____
just so man - y things
Noth - ing's fine, ___ } I'm torn. _
that I ___ can't touch, _

___ I'm ___ all out of faith, ___ this ___ is how _ I feel. _

___ I'm cold and I ___ am shamed _ ly - ing na -

- ked on ___ the floor. ___ Il - lu - sion nev - er changed _

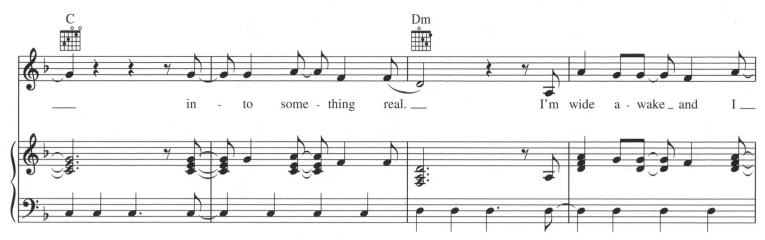

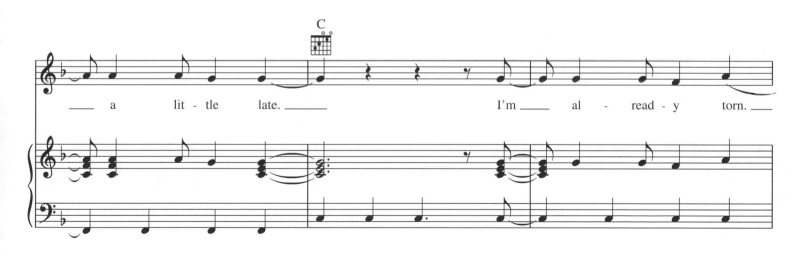

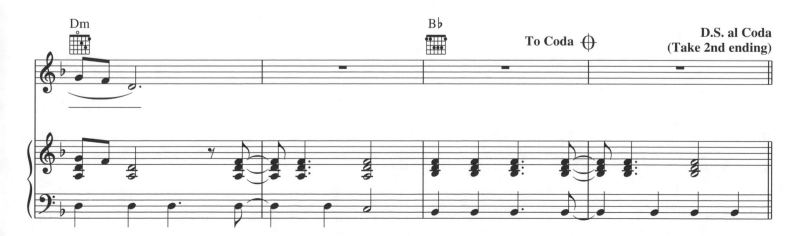

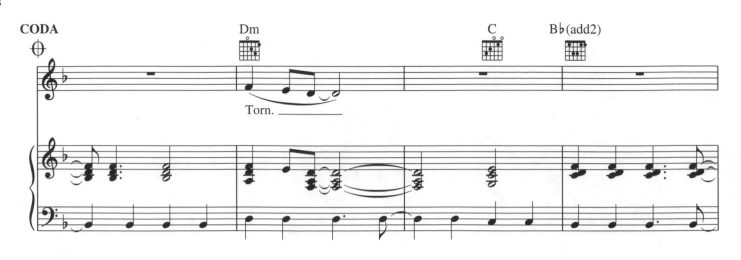

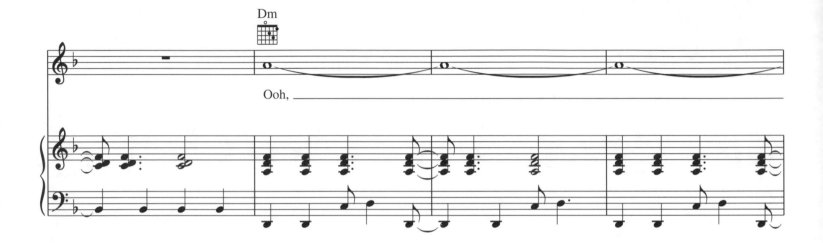

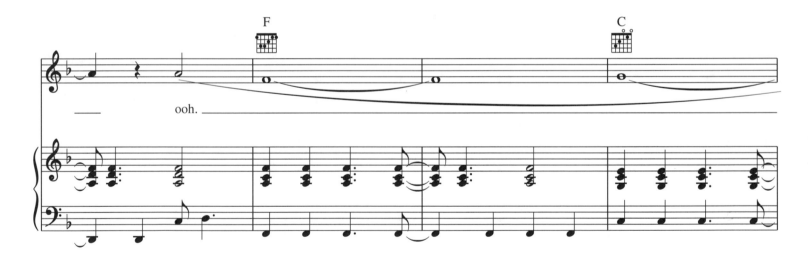

has run dry. That's what's go-ing on. ___ Noth -

- ing's right,_ I'm torn. ___ I'm ___ all out of faith, ___ this_

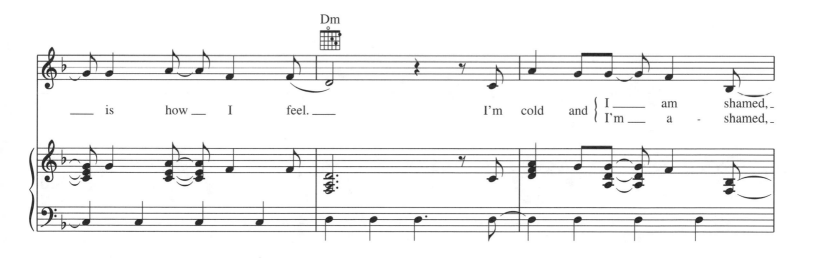

___ is how ___ I feel. ___ I'm cold and { I___ am shamed,_ / I'm___ a - shamed,_

ly - ing na - ked on ___ the floor. ___ Il - lu -
bound and bro - ken on ___ the floor. ___ You're_

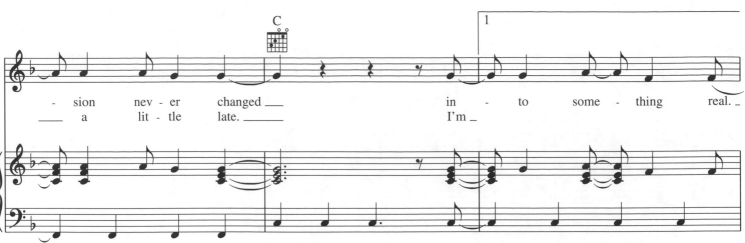

-sion nev-er changed ___ in-to some-thing real. ___
___ a lit-tle late. ___ I'm ___

___ I'm wide a-wake ___ and I ___ can see ___ the per-

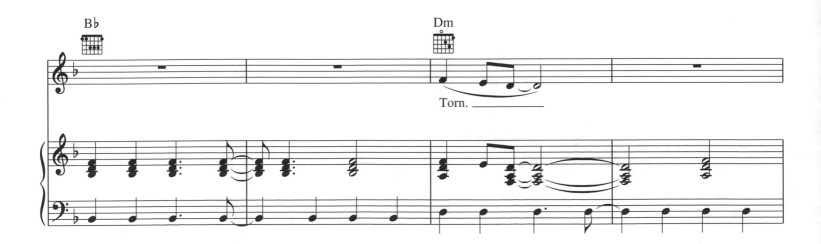

-fect sky ___ is torn. ___ al-read-y torn. ___

Torn. ___

Torn. _____

Guitar solo - ad lib.

TUBTHUMPING

Words and Music by NIGEL HUNTER, BRUCE DUNCAN, ALICE NUTTER, LOUISE WATTS,
PAUL GRECO, DARREN HAMER, ALLEN WHALLEY and JUDITH ABBOTT

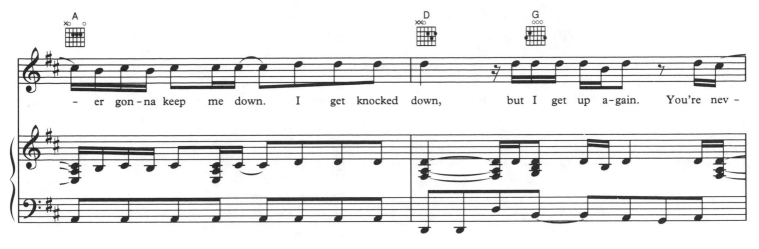

- er gon-na keep me down. I get knocked down, but I get up a-gain. You're nev-

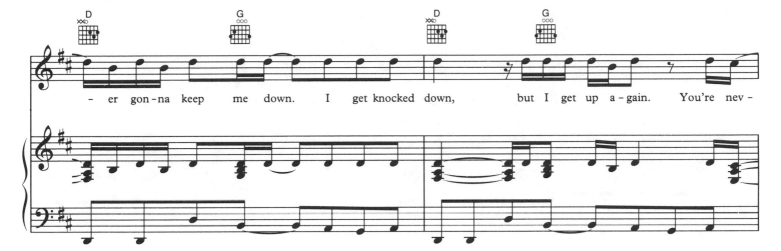

- er gon-na keep me down. I get knocked down, but I get up a-gain. You're nev-

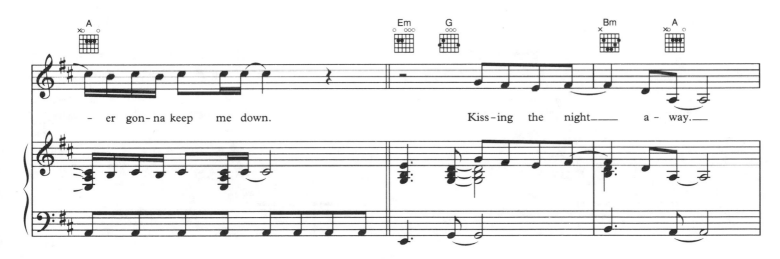

- er gon-na keep me down. Kiss-ing the night____ a - way.____

Kiss - ing the night____ a - way.____ He drinks a

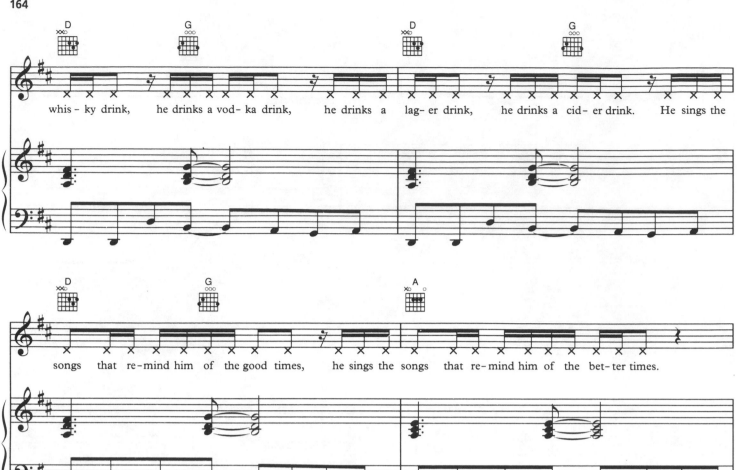

whis-ky drink, he drinks a vod-ka drink, he drinks a lag-er drink, he drinks a cid-er drink. He sings the

songs that re-mind him of the good times, he sings the songs that re-mind him of the bet-ter times.

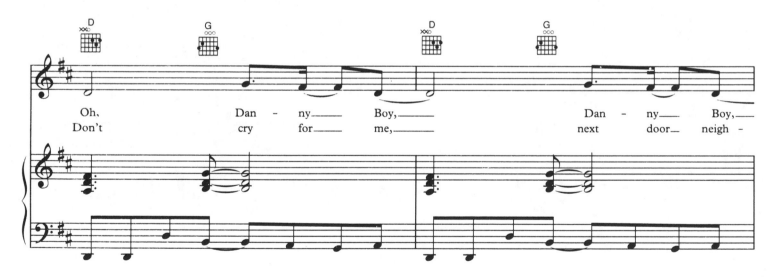

Oh, Dan - ny____ Boy,____ Dan - ny__ Boy,____
Don't cry for____ me,____ next door__ neigh -

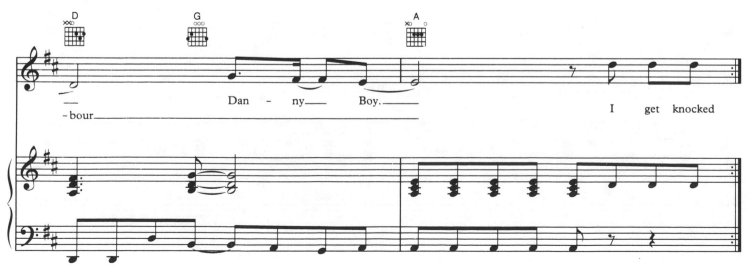

- bour____ Dan - ny__ Boy.____ I get knocked

down, but I get up a-gain. You're nev – er gon-na keep me down.

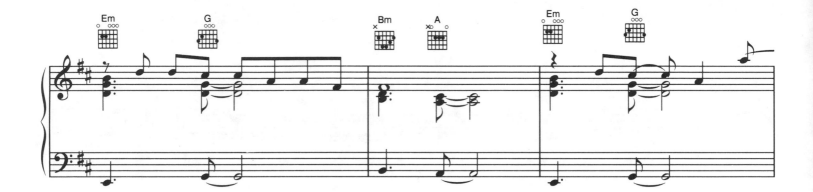

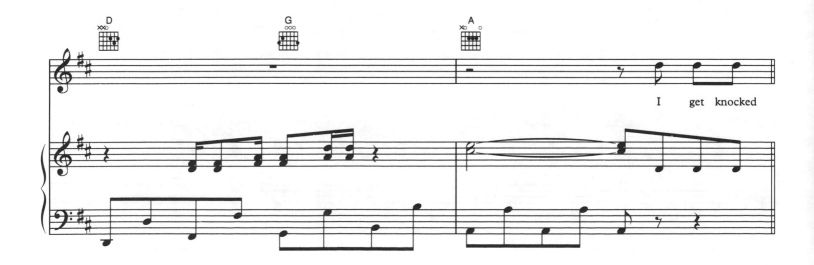

I get knocked

down, but I get up a-gain. You're nev - er gon-na keep me down. I get knocked

down, but I get up a-gain. You're nev - er gon-na keep me down. I get knocked

down, but I get up a-gain. You're nev - er gon-na keep me down.__ I get knocked

repeat and fade

down, but I get up a-gain. You're nev - er gon-na keep me down. I get knocked

YOU'RE STILL THE ONE

Words and Music by SHANIA TWAIN
and R.J. LANGE

UNINVITED
from the Motion Picture CITY OF ANGELS

Words and Music by
ALANIS MORISSETTE

Slowly

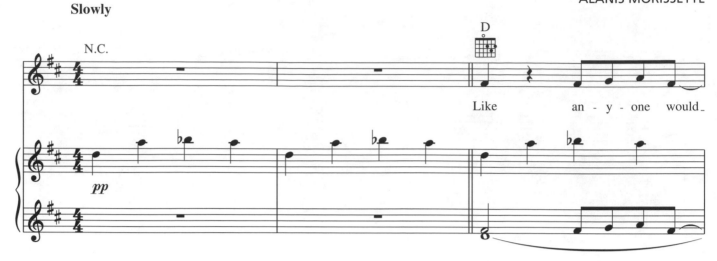

Like an-y-one would be, I am flat-tered by your fas-ci-na-tion with me.

Like an-y hot-blood-ed wo-man, I have simp-ly

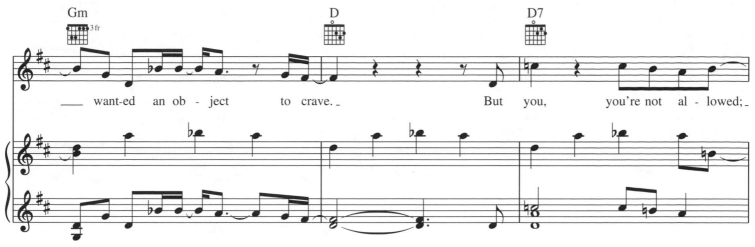

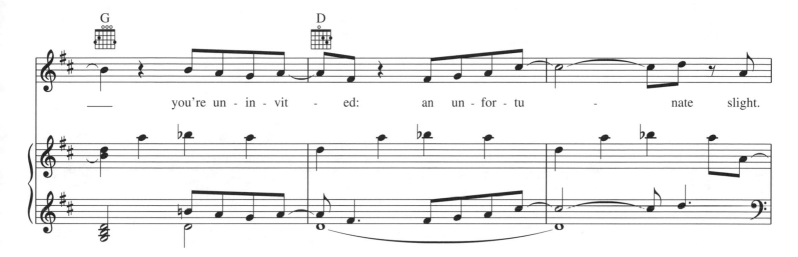

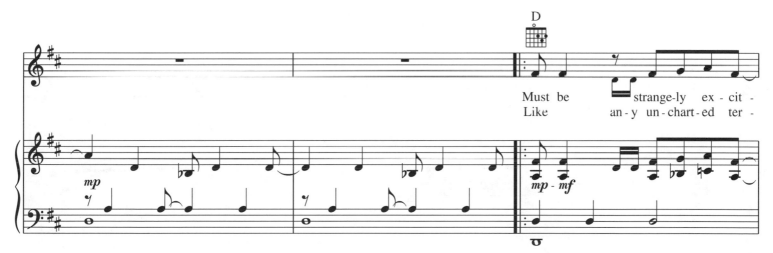

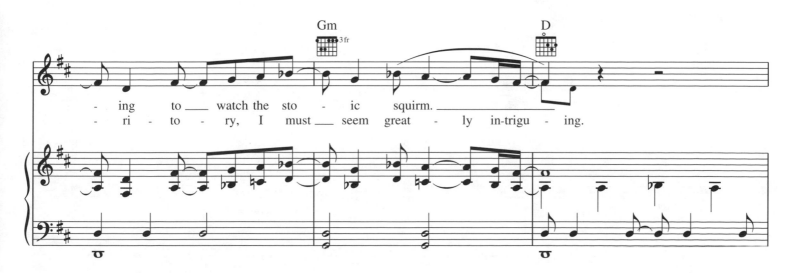

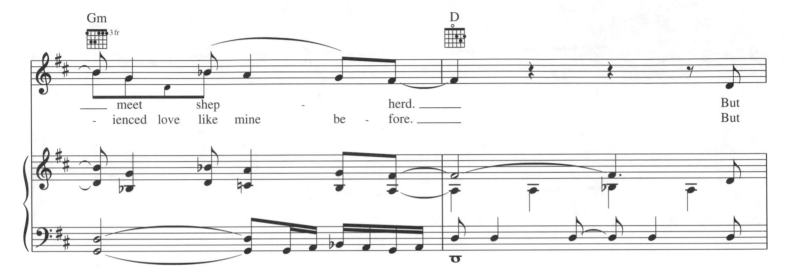

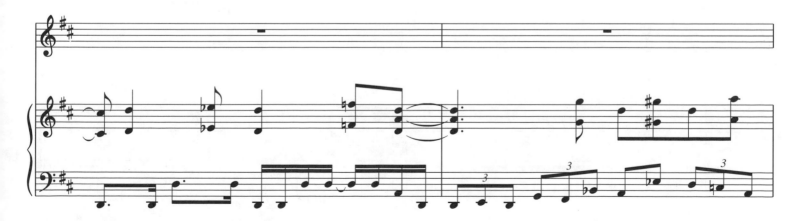

I don't think you un-wor - thy; I need a mo -

Gm   D

- ment to de-lib-er - ate. _____   *Guitar solo ad lib.*

Play 4 times   D5